Life Cycle of A Christian
A User's Guide To Life After Rebirth!

Thanks for joining us in worship today! I hope "Life Cycle" will help you grow in your walk with Jesus! See you next Sunday!

Grace and peace,

Pastor Chris

Dr. Chris E. Marshall

LIFE CYCLE OF A CHRISTIAN:
A User's Guide to Life After Rebirth

© 2008 by Chris E. Marshall
International Standard Book Number: 9780615233130

Printed in the United States by The Eagle Printery
Butler, Pennsylvania

For Information:
Dr. Chris E. Marshall
447 Leasureville Road
Cabot, PA 16023
CMarsh1957@aol.com

I dedicate this book to Andy Wiegand
my first Mentor
and first Jesus follower
who made me want to follow Jesus, too!

Acknowledgements

First, I thank Jesus for giving me the new life that only he could provide. Without that amazing gift, nothing else in life would matter.

I want to thank Nancy, my wife, for being my number one encourager over my twenty-four years in parish ministry. Long before that she brought much needed focus and discipline to my life and made it possible for me to pursue my seminary education, by putting her career on hold to work to provide for our family so I could pursue God's call in my life. Thanks for being the "rudder" for our family through nearly thirty years of married life!

Thanks to Abby and Emmy, the two best daughters any dad could ever have. You have challenged me "not to preach what I'm not going to do" over the years, and made me aware of the many times when my words and actions needed to be brought closer together. Thanks to Emmy for some great final editing for *Life Cycle,* as well.

Thanks to the LIFE(Living in Faith Everyday) Groups at New Life for using *Life Cycle* in your home groups, and giving me some valuable real life input to it.

Thanks to Lisa Johns for editing and formatting suggestions for *Life Cycle.* I know you gave a great gift—the gift of time—in reviewing and revising both the content and final "look" of the book. I'm grateful for your expertise.

Thanks to Brad French for the original idea for the cover design, and to Debbie Heist of the Eagle Printery for the final design.

Finally, thanks to Karen Wise of the Eagle Printery for her encouragement, advice, expertise and faith in seeing that *Life Cycle* became a reality.

Life Cycle of a Christian: A User's Guide to Life After Rebirth

Contents

Introduction

For many years now, I have been bouncing a question around in my mind: Why do some Christians "grow" while others seem to stagnate or even "backslide" for decades? As I have pondered that question, asked others what they think, and prayed about it at some length, the matter has become clearer: *Some Christians grow and others do not because growth for followers of Jesus is "optional."* We must choose to grow. We must commit to grow. We must give control of the growth process over to God. As we do those things, growth takes place as naturally as grass grows, as fruit trees bear fruit, as you and I progress through the stages of physical life—birth, infancy, childhood, adolescence, adulthood and, ultimately, death. If we do not make the choice to grow, if we do not commit to growth, if we do not give control of our growth over to God, then a year from now, a decade from now, a **century** from now, we will be in the same place spiritually that we are at **this** moment.

The Life Cycle of a Christian gives you the opportunity to examine the "stages" of growth in a follower of Jesus' life from "birth" to standing in the presence of Jesus. To be sure, it is possible for a believer to be "born again," to stay in a state of spiritual infancy and then eventually to stand in the presence of Jesus without maturing at all; but that is not Jesus' plan for believers! He wants us to grow in every way into maturity, just as He did. In these pages, you have the opportunity to read and study on your own. If you do that—calling on God to give you wisdom and understanding as you invest time and energy in the process—you **will** see what growth looks like for Jesus' followers, you will be challenged to grow, and you will grow. If, in addition to reading and studying on your own, you also join with others to engage in the same process in regular times of discussion, reflection, prayer and commitment to action, you will grow even more! My prayer and goal for you and for everyone who reads, studies, and lives out *The Life Cycle of a Christian* is that you will grow up into the full stature of Jesus. As you do that you will commit to passing on the fully devoted life in Jesus to others, because Jesus calls His followers not only to grow themselves, but also to make disciples of all nations.

One final, practical suggestion: You may want to read this book as you do most books: starting at the beginning and reading through to the end. After you do that, read it again <u>over at least a ten-week period</u>. Each week, as you read a chapter, engage yourself (and others!) in the Questions For Discussion And Growth at the end of each chapter. **Most of all, ACT on what you read.** It has been said that information without application is abortion. The statement is strong but true. Jesus said the same thing in a "softer" way in John 13:17, "Now that you know these things [Jesus' teachings], you will be blessed if you **do** them!" (NIV, emphasis added)

May God bless you richly as you work your way through *The Life Cycle of a Christian* and may you be a blessing to others as you apply and pass what you learn on to them!

Pastor Chris Marshall, Senior Pastor
New Life Christian Ministries
Saxonburg, PA 16056
www.newlifexn.org

1

Born Again

³Jesus replied, "I tell you the truth, unless you are born again, you cannot see the Kingdom of God." John 3:3 NLT

Introduction: Born Once, Die Twice...

Back on March 31, 2001, I met Mr. Earl McRoberts for the first time. Earl and others had built a worship center for the Bible Church of Ivywood, a church he had started in his living room, in the 1950s. For many years, people had gathered there to worship and serve in Jesus' name, however on that day, the building had stood empty for a couple years. Earl's grandson, David, had called to let me know of the building's availability the day before. I had recently left a ministry of many years in the Presbyterian Church, USA, as God was calling me in a new direction. David suggested the new church—New Life Christian Ministries—might be able to meet in the old Ivywood Church building. He arranged a meeting for me with his grandfather for the next morning.

As Earl walked into the building at 8:30 that last morning in March, he needed a cane to steady his body; but his spirit required no steadying! Earl and I exchanged greetings; and after a relatively brief discussion, he offered us the use of the building as a place for our new congregation to worship and grow. At the moment the "congregation" consisted only of my immediate family and an undetermined number of like-minded folks who would also follow God's call to move in a new direction. The next Sunday morning, as folks arrived for our first, official worship service as New Life Christian Ministries, Earl and Rose, his wife of many decades, came in and chose a pew about half way back in the sanctuary. Tears flowed down Earl's face as more and more people arrived filling the room to participate in worship, the purpose for which he and others had built it so many years before.

After the service, I noticed Earl was wearing a small button on his lapel. It read: "Born once, die twice.

Born twice, die once."

I had never seen that clear, simple description of the profound reality we all face. If we are only born **physically**, then we will die **physically** *and* we will die **spiritually**. On the other hand, if we are born **physically** *and* **spiritually**, then we will die **physically** but go on to enjoy eternal life with God in heaven!

Born once, die twice. Born twice, die once. What an apt introduction to our first topic! Here we reflect on what it means to be born again. Even in Christian circles, the phrase *born again* triggers much discussion and disagreement. For some, the phrase is old-fashioned or offensive. Since Jesus coined it, we will use it here. After all, Jesus told us unless we are born again, we will never see (or enter) the Kingdom of God. In our reading and discussion, we will consider what it really means to be "born twice." We will acknowledge that the life cycle of **every** Christian starts with being born again. (Sadly, for some it ends there as well!) We will underline the new birth as the essential starting point in every believer's life cycle. We will also make certain every reader understands how to be "born twice," since being born twice is the **only** way to guarantee that we only die once!

For the Questions For Discussion And Growth for *Introduction: Born Once, Die Twice* go to page 14 now!

Jesus' Teaching on Rebirth (John 3:1-8)

The biblical basis for the phrase *born again* comes directly from the mouth of Jesus. In His discussion with the Jewish religious teacher, Nicodemus, Jesus set forth the reality that for a person to proceed along the life cycle of a Christian (although He did not use those words) the first step is being born again. Look at what Jesus said in John 3:1-8:

> [1]There was a man named Nicodemus, a Jewish religious leader who was a Pharisee. [2]After dark one evening, he came to speak with Jesus. "Rabbi," he said, "we all know that God has sent you to teach us. Your miraculous signs are evidence that God is with you."
>
> [3]Jesus replied, "I tell you the truth, unless you are born again, you cannot see the Kingdom of God."
>
> [4]"What do you mean?" exclaimed Nicodemus. "How can an old man go back into his mother's womb and be born again?"
>
> [5]Jesus replied, "I assure you, no one can enter the Kingdom of God without being born of water and the Spirit. [6]Humans can reproduce only human life, but the Holy Spirit gives birth to spiritual life. [7]So don't be surprised when I say, 'You must be born again.' [8]The wind blows wherever it wants. Just as you can hear the wind but can't tell where it comes from or where it is going, so you can't explain how people are born of the Spirit." (John 3:1-8 NLT)

Jesus made it clear that there is a **beginning** to the life of a follower of Jesus. That beginning is so radical He called it being "born again." Some scholars suggest the Greek text allows for the translation "born from above" rather than "born again." Indeed, it does, but the context does not. How does Nicodemus respond to Jesus' statement, "I tell you the truth, unless you are born again, you cannot see the Kingdom of God"?

He asks, [4]"What do you mean… How can an old man go back into his mother's womb and be born again?" Obviously, Nicodemus understood that Jesus was telling him the way to enter the Kingdom of God was to be **born again**. Jesus went on to explain to Nicodemus that the new birth consists of receiving the Holy Spirit. The second birth is a spiritual birth. When Jesus said we must be born of water and the Spirit, He made it clear that we are born physically of water and spiritually of the Spirit. **The second birth is not universal.** However, it is the prerequisite for entering the Kingdom of God. As we consider the life cycle of a Christian we see that it starts with birth. That birth is available to all who will receive it. Being born again means nothing more or less than the Spirit of God coming into us in response to our acceptance of Jesus' lordship and salvation in our lives. How does that happen? Jesus told us the new birth is something of a mystery. In fact, He said, "Just as you can hear the wind but can't tell where it comes from or where it is going, so you can't explain how people are born of the Spirit." Jesus tells us that how one is born again cannot be reduced to a formula. This much is clear from Scripture: We are born again by confessing that Jesus Christ is Lord and by believing that God raised Him from the dead. (See Romans 10:9-10.)

Being born again happens in an instant, just as physical birth happens in an instant. However, just as physical birth is a process that sometimes takes many hours, being born again is a process that may also take a **long** time. The growth process after birth is what distinguishes the spiritual life from the physical life. Physical growth takes place naturally and progressively. *Spiritual growth takes place supernaturally and must be pursued intentionally!* Jesus tells us we must be born again in order to enter the Kingdom of God. Thus, if we want to experience eternal life, we must be born again. Being born again is not optional for any who would experience the new life Jesus offers.

For the Questions For Discussion And Growth for
Jesus' Teaching On Rebirth go to page 15 now!

Born-Again Christians

Have you ever been asked whether you are a "born-again Christian"? I have many times. Every time I am asked, I smile and say, "Yes, I am." Inside, I want to say more, but I usually do not. I want to say, "The phrase 'born-again Christian' is redundant." In order to be a Christian at all, Jesus tells us we must be born again. Actually, Jesus never told us we must become "Christians." Followers of Jesus were originally called "The Way." A number of years went by after Jesus' death, resurrection and ascension into heaven, before his followers became known as Christians. The point, though, is in order to be a follower of Jesus—and thus a Christian— one **must** be born again. To call one a Christian who has not been born again is problematic at best. After all, if Jesus said in order to enter the Kingdom of God we **must** be born again (and He did), then to be a Christian would mean being born again at the very least. Here is the point: To call someone a *born-again Christian* is really to call the person a *Christian Christian*.

I know that folks such as George Barna have identified "born-again Christians" as those who subscribe to a certain specific set of doctrinal truths (i.e., Jesus being born of a virgin, His being sinless, His having died on the cross and risen from the grave and being the only means through whom a person may enter heaven). For our purposes, though, the **starting** point for the life cycle of a Christian is being born again. It is affirming Jesus' command that we **must** be born again. So, from here on out, we will assume that those who are born again **are** Christians and those who are Christians **are** born again! The next time someone asks you whether you are a "born-again

Christian" just say "yes" and smile as you think about being called a Christian Christian!

For the Questions For Discussion And Growth for
Born Again Christians go to page 16 now!

Anyone Who Belongs To Christ (2 Corinthians 5:17-21)

Another important Scripture as we consider the new birth the starting point in the life cycle of a Christian is the Apostle Paul's teaching found in 2 Corinthians 5:17-21:

> [17]This means that anyone who belongs to Christ has become a new person. The old life is gone; a new life has begun! [18]And all of this is a gift from God, who brought us back to himself through Christ. And God has given us this task of reconciling people to him. [19]For God was in Christ, reconciling the world to himself, no longer counting people's sins against them. And he gave us this wonderful message of reconciliation. [20]So we are Christ's ambassadors; God is making his appeal through us. We speak for Christ when we plead, "Come back to God!" [21]For God made Christ, who never sinned, to be the offering for our sin, so that we could be made right with God through Christ. (2 Corinthians 5:17-21 NLT)

How incredible is that! "**Anyone** who belongs to Jesus Christ has become a new person" (emphasis added). Paul goes so far as to say "…the old life is **gone**; a new life has begun!" (emphasis added). As any of us who have received that new life are aware, the old life does not go away easily. In fact, one of the main reasons people stall in their growth along the life cycle of a Christian is they believe such growth comes automatically. I know I did. I was born again when I was twelve, and I thought that from that moment, I would never be

10

able to sin again. I thought Jesus would change my thoughts, words and actions in an instant. He did not! As we have said, the new birth is instantaneous; but growth requires intentionality or it will not take place at all. The old life **is** gone, as Paul tells us, but the new life has only **begun**. Growing up in Jesus is a process, not an event. As we will see, living as followers of Jesus means investing our lives in Him.

After Paul tells us of the new life we receive, he goes on to say not only that this life is a gift from God—meaning we cannot earn it—but that God has also given us the task, or as some translations state it the **ministry** of reconciliation. From the moment of our new birth, we become "ambassadors for Christ." God makes His appeal to the world through us from that moment. That is another incredible truth! I bring it up here because Paul linked our ministry inextricably to our new birth. In order for us, as followers of Jesus, to be His ambassadors, all we have to do is be born again. **However, in order for us to be *effective* ambassadors for Jesus Christ, we must grow up fully in Him.** Neither Jesus nor Paul nor any other New Testament writer believed that being reborn was the completion of the life cycle of a Christian. Each of them saw it as the starting point. Unlike newborn babies in the physical realm, who take years before they are able to do things for themselves, even newborn followers of Jesus have the capacity to love, serve Jesus and grow. May we be encouraged by the affirmation of our call to ministry through our new birth, and may we be challenged to keep growing so we will be more and more effective ambassadors for Jesus with each passing day!

For the Questions For Discussion And Growth for
Anyone Who Belongs To Christ go to page 16 now!

A New and Eternal Life (1 Peter 1:22-23)

We move now to our final Scripture that focuses on the importance of being born again. These words are found in the Apostle Peter's first letter to the Church:

> [22]You were cleansed from your sins when you obeyed the truth, so now you must show sincere love to each other as brothers and sisters. Love each other deeply with all your heart. [23]For you have been born again, but not to a life that will quickly end. Your new life will last forever because it comes from the eternal, living word of God. (1 Peter 1:22-23 NLT)

Peter linked being born again with the cleansing of our lives from sin and demonstrating sincere love to one another as brothers and sisters in Jesus. One of the most important reminders this brief Scripture offers us is that being born again means becoming part of God's family. When we are born again, we gain many brothers and sisters, not only those in the local church we call home, but also in the Church of Jesus Christ around the world, and of all time! Peter tells us our new birth is not to a life "that will quickly end." Our new life is eternal. Just as Jesus made it clear to Nicodemus that being born again is the prerequisite for eternal life, Peter reiterated to his readers that being born again assures we will only die once. Then we live with God forever! Some have said that life is short. We need to amend that statement: **This** life is short, but each of us faces eternity at the end of this life. Facing eternity without being born again means being separated from God forever. But once we have been born again, we are assured of living our lives with God now, and with Him and an immense family of brothers and sisters through Jesus Christ forever.

Here is the million dollar question: Have you been born again? Have you been cleansed from your sins as you "obeyed the truth," to use Peter's words? If you have, then praise the Lord! That new life is forever. If you have not been born again, or if you are not sure whether you have, there is no time like now to make sure. Jesus never told us to accept Him, to receive Him or to pray a "sinner's prayer." What He told us was to **confess** Him. To confess Him as Jesus used the word literally means to "say the same thing" or to agree with Jesus. With what does Jesus want us to agree? He wants us to agree that we have sinned. He wants us to agree that we have walked in darkness (sin) and avoided the light (His life). (See John 3:16-20) He wants us to trust Him—and Him alone—to control our lives. In biblical terms He wants to be our Savior and Lord. Many **have** prayed a sinner's prayer, which may have been worded like this:

Lord, Jesus, I confess to You that I am a sinner. I have not done Your will in my life. Right now, I turn away from my sins and ask You to forgive me. I ask You to come into my life and become my Savior and Lord. Fill me with Your Holy Spirit. I thank You for Your life and love, which is for today and for eternity. In Jesus' name, I pray. Amen.

Is that what it means to be born again? Yes or No. Yes, if you truly acknowledge that you are a sinner, that you have broken God's law and deserve His just punishment—separation from Him forever in hell. Yes, if you receive Jesus' payment for that sin, His death on the cross of Calvary and the new life He offers by His Spirit. On the other hand, No if you offer the prayer simply to get some Christian off your back or if you see it merely as a free ticket to heaven. How do you know whether it is Yes or No? The Yes moves forward. The Yes seeks to become more and more like Jesus—not without failures and difficulties—but with a commitment to becoming more and more like Jesus. The No does not change. Weeks, months, years after praying the prayer, an outside observer sees no apparent change, no transformation, nothing different at all. Jesus once told His followers, "Not everyone who says, 'Lord, Lord,' will enter the Kingdom of Heaven, but only those who do the will of my Father in heaven."

(Matthew 7:21 NIV) He was not telling us that salvation is based on our efforts. He was telling us the new birth is evidenced by growth. I said at the outset a person could be born again, and then live for many years and end up in the presence of God, without having grown at all as a follower of Jesus. That is true, because God's grace in Jesus Christ is all that is necessary for our salvation. At the same time, we know beyond any doubt, because of the words of Matthew 7:21, that followers of Jesus who remain infants throughout their lives as Christians do not honor Jesus or fulfill His plan for their lives.

Jesus calls for a response. He calls us to confess Him before God and others. Let us be challenged and encouraged to grow up in every way into Him who is the head of the body—Jesus! Let us grow bolder and more joyous in our confessions of Jesus as Savior and Lord; and as we do, may we draw others to Him as well!

For the Questions For Discussion And Growth for
A New And Eternal Life go to page 17 now!

Questions For Discussion And Growth

Introduction: Born Once, Die Twice

Had you ever heard the expression "Born once, die twice. Born twice, die once," before reading the introduction to this chapter? If so, when and where?

What does the saying mean to you?

What would you say to someone who says that the idea of being born twice is absurd? (Remember, **how** we say something is often as important as what we say--especially if we are disagreeing with someone for whom Jesus died!)

Jesus' Teaching On Rebirth (John 3:1-8)

Why do you suppose Nicodemus came to Jesus for spiritual advice, even though he belonged to a religious establishment that rejected Jesus?

What does Jesus' statement that we must be "born again" mean to you?

Why do you suppose some people in the Christian Community are uncomfortable with the phrase "born again"?

Born-Again Christians

Have you ever been asked whether you are a born-again Christian? If so, how have you responded?

What do you make of the statement that the phrase "born-again Christian" is redundant? Do you agree or disagree? Why?

Anyone Who Belongs To Christ

Do you see being "born again" and "becoming a new person" as synonymous? Why or why not?

What does it mean for you to be an "ambassador" for Christ? How do you live that out each day?

A New And Eternal Life

What is the connection between loving one another and being born again?

Is praying a "sinner's prayer" a certainty that a person has been born again? Why or why not?

What is the most important truth you have learned from this first chapter?

2

Babes In Christ

You are like babies who need milk and cannot eat solid food. [13]For someone who lives on milk is still an infant and doesn't know how to do what is right. [14]Solid food is for those who are mature, who through training have the skill to recognize the difference between right and wrong. Hebrews 11:12b-14 NLT

Introduction: *Bios* vs. *Zoe*

In the Greek language used in Jesus' day, we find two different words translated as *life*: *bios (βίος)* and *zoe (ζωη)*. As we consider the life cycle of a Christian, these words shed light on our topic. The word *bios* is used in the New Testament to refer to physical or biological life, while the word *zoe* is used to refer to spiritual life. In John 10:10, when Jesus says, "[10]The thief comes only to steal and kill and destroy; I have come that they may have life, and have it to the full," (John 10:10 NIV), the life to which He refers is *zoe*. Jesus did not come merely to give us the best physical life we can live. Many times following Jesus can be quite disruptive to our physical lives! Jesus' goal is to give us the life that is truly life—the unending life of the Spirit. We could say that after we are born again, we have *zoe*. We still have *bios*, of course; but now God lives in us by means of the Holy Spirit. That empowers us to grow through infancy and childhood toward maturity in our life cycle as a Christian. We cannot overestimate the importance of the distinction here. *Zoe* is not natural life. It is God's life within us. As we grow in Him, as we become healthy in Him, the process of spiritual growth moves forward. It always requires intentionality, unlike *bios*, which happens whether we want it to or not. As we put God first in our lives, growth occurs. Here in chapter two, we consider several Scriptures, which help us see both what it means to be a "babe in Christ" and how the process of growth continues. While each Scripture has a different emphasis, each gives us an important perspective on moving from *bios* thinking and living to *zoe* thinking and living.

For the Questions For Discussion And Growth for *Introduction:* Bios *vs.* Zoe go to page 26 now!

The Walk Begins

The famous Chinese believer, Watchman Nee, once wrote a book about the Apostle Paul's letter to the church at Ephesus titled *Sit, Walk, Stand.* In it, Nee shows the reader how Paul structured His letter to point out that the Christian life consists of "sitting" in the heavenlies with Jesus, "walking" with Him in our daily lives, and "standing" firm against the devil. Nee saw a progression in our walk with Jesus. The starting point, what we are referring to as *infancy*, Nee referred to as "sitting" with Jesus. In order for us to walk or grow with Jesus, we must be born again and then learn the rudimentary principles of our faith in Him, which we may liken to Nee's "sitting" or infancy. Some folks never move past this stage as they develop as Jesus' followers. How sad it is when Jesus gives us a new life—one that is truly life—and, instead of investing all we can into growing up in that life, we remain babies. Sometimes we become "stuck" as babies because we do not have instruction. Sometimes we become stuck because we do have instruction but do not commit to living it out in our daily lives. Sometimes the world's ways put obstacles in front of us. The pursuit of a successful *bios* often gets in the way of a significant *zoe*. The key in moving from infancy to childhood in the life cycle of a Christian is to remember that spiritual life and growth is supernatural. It does not happen automatically or accidentally. Only when we call on Jesus to fill us with the Holy Spirit, and then give Him control, will we grow spiritually. One of the best parts of spiritual life is we do not have to stay infants for long! Our growth can occur at an incredible rate if we simply let Jesus lead in our lives.

I once met a man who was in his late sixties. He had not been born again until he was in his early sixties. I did not know that. From the maturity of his walk with Jesus, I assumed he had been a believer for decades. I was amazed when he told me he had only known the Lord for such a short time. That kind of rapid growth is available to each of us, but we must devote ourselves to Jesus to experience it. Infancy takes a more or less fixed length of time in the physical realm, but thank God we can breeze right through it when we are born again. All we have to do is trust in the Lord and live in the presence and power of His Spirit. Then growth will proceed at a dramatic pace. A number of "environmental factors" will speed our growth toward maturity as well. They include: fervent prayer; reading and studying God's word diligently and consistently while applying its truth to our daily lives; mentors; participating in a God-honoring body of believers; giving generously; participating in ministry and mission as much as we can; and telling others of our abiding relationship with Jesus!

For the Questions For Discussion And Growth for *The Walk Begins* go to page 26 now!

Learning to Lean on God (Proverbs 3:5-6)

The starting point in our growth from infancy is learning to "lean on" or trust God. Since many of us have been taught from infancy that the goal of life (*bios*) is to become **independent,** the concept of leaning on anyone, even God, challenges us. We are taught to make our own choices and decisions. If that has been our experience, when we are born again we may find it extremely difficult to give up control of our lives to God. King Solomon, often considered to be the wisest man who ever lived until the birth of Jesus, helps us understand the process of growth in the life cycle of a Christian. He wrote that it begins with offering God the trust we find so hard to give: "[5]Trust in the LORD with all your heart and lean not on your own understanding; [6]in all your ways acknowledge him, and he will make your paths straight" (Proverbs 3:5-6 NIV).

Notice that Solomon told us to trust in the Lord with all of our **heart**, not all of our mind, not all of our will. In fact, he made it clear that we are not to lean on our "own understanding," that is on our minds. Solomon was not telling us that growing as a follower of God means never using our minds. He was telling us that trusting God is more important than understanding. Sometimes, actually **many** times, in our growth as Jesus' followers, we will be led to think, say and do things that seem contrary to common sense, popular opinion, or what the world has taught is right or expedient. At those times we have to make a choice: Will we lean on God or our own understanding? Theologian Emil Brunner once said God is not "illogical" but sometimes God is "alogical." Do you see the difference? God is not foolish. God does not ask us to do things that are against logic, but sometimes He does ask us to do things that are beyond human logic! Solomon points out how far our allegiance and trust in God must go when he says, "In **all** your ways acknowledge Him" (emphasis added). In these moments we either grow or remain infants. When God says, "Speak up for me right now—right now in the middle of this meeting," we are faced with a choice—actually with several choices. We can ask, "Is God really directing me here or is it my imagination?" We can argue with God, "Not now, God.

Don't you see that if I speak up right now, I'll suffer the consequences of being thought a fanatic or worse?" We can take back control and say, "God, you can be in charge of my Sunday mornings but not here at work." What we do in such situations determines whether we grow or remain "babes in Christ." The starting point for growth is to trust God with all our hearts and to acknowledge Him in all our ways. The Scripture promises when we do that God will direct our paths, or to put it another way—God will move us from infancy to the next step in our maturity!

For the Questions For Discussion And Growth for
Learning To Lean On God go to page 27 now!

Moving Beyond Milk (Hebrews 5:11-14)

The author of the letter to the Hebrews (many assume it was the Apostle Paul) offers a blunt statement about followers of Jesus who fail to mature. Given that these believers lived no more than a few decades after Jesus walked the earth, we can be sure that nearly 2,000 years later believers still struggle with the same challenge: failure to grow in our spirits! Look at what the author says and challenges his readers to do:

> [11]We have much to say about this, but it is hard to explain because you are slow to learn. [12]In fact, though by this time you ought to be teachers, you need someone to teach you the elementary truths of God's word all over again. You need milk, not solid food! [13]Anyone who lives on milk, being still an infant, is not acquainted with the teaching about righteousness. [14]But solid food is for the mature, who by constant use have trained themselves to distinguish good from evil. (Hebrews 5:11-14 NIV)

Consider this: How long had these believers been born again? They are told they ought to be teachers by this time; instead, they were still "babies." The reality is they could not have been believers for too long, since Jesus had lived only a few decades before! Apparently, the life cycle of a Christian is supposed to progress from infancy to maturity rapidly—much more rapidly than the biological processes of life. I remember when I first became a pastor; I was twenty-seven years old. In the church where I served as a youth pastor, people twice my age would defer to my answers because I had gone to seminary. That always surprised me. If someone has been a believer for thirty or forty years or more, then how could a twenty-seven year old be more mature in Jesus? The answer is simple: *Chronological passage of time does not guarantee spiritual growth and maturity.* (Attendance in a seminary does not guarantee it either!) The words we read from Hebrews 5:11-14 remind us that growth is **assumed** by the author, yet he acknowledged that the growth he assumed was not taking place. Instead of mature believers, who could teach others, they were still "drinking milk."

How long did you "drink milk"? Are you still drinking it? Have you matured? Are you teaching others the truths of Scripture? Many have found that when they are called to instruct others on matters of faith, their own understanding grows. I know I always learn a great deal when I am asked to teach or preach because such activity requires prayer, digging into God's word and considering the action potential of a passage so the message presents a challenge to growth or a call to action worth pursuing. After all, only when we act on the truth of God's word do we mature from spiritual milk to solid food! The final words of this Scripture tell us how we know we are maturing: *We can distinguish between good and evil.* In our day, many folks have come to believe there is no distinction between good and evil; but there always has been and still is. As we grow in our maturity as believers, we become more and more adept at discerning good from evil. We learn how to help others see the difference as well. Spiritual growth is essential if we are going to influence the world for good in Jesus' name.

For the Questions For Discussion And Growth for
Moving Beyond Milk go to page 28 now!

Craving Spiritual Milk (1 Peter 2:1-3)

Our final Scripture in this chapter reminds us of one crucial **positive** of being babes in Christ: Newborns **crave** milk. Although it has been a long time, I remember our daughters Abby and Emmy as newborns screaming in the middle of the night because they were hungry. The Apostle Peter uses this truth as an analogy to point out how we grow as followers of Jesus:

> [1]Therefore, rid yourselves of all malice and all deceit, hypocrisy, envy, and slander of every kind. [2]Like newborn babies, crave pure spiritual milk, so that by it you may grow up in your salvation, [3]now that you have tasted that the Lord is good. (1 Peter 2:1-3 NIV)

The key statement is "**Like** newborn babies, **crave pure spiritual milk**" (emphasis added). Why? So we may grow up in our salvation! Peter reminds us we have tasted that the Lord is good. This truth often escapes the notice of the world and, many times, even those who know Jesus. Are we like newborn babies craving pure spiritual milk when it comes to our growth as His followers?

I remember when I first trusted Jesus as my Savior and Lord. For a while, I could not get enough of the Bible. I read it all the time. After a while, that craving seemed to fade. Why? Had I learned it all? Of course not! Distractions wedged their way between the word and me. Thankfully, Andy Wiegand came along a few years later and invested time in studying God's word with me. Once again, the Bible came to life and I craved it like a newborn baby craving pure spiritual milk. During that time, my growth proceeded rapidly once again.

24

Over the years, I have experienced similar growth spurts along the way. Have you experienced that? Have you found certain times, situations or mentors who helped you move from one stage in the life cycle of a Christian to another? I hope so. If you have not, I pray the Apostle Peter's words will move you to a time of craving the pure spiritual milk so you, too, may grow up in your salvation.

Let me emphasize again what Peter pointed to as the source of our craving: We have already tasted and found that the Lord is good. So many people think following Jesus is boring, irrelevant, old-fashioned or weak. Nothing could be farther from the truth. Sometimes followers of Jesus cause people to hold disparaging ideas of what it means to follow Him. We have failed to live with the passion and zeal that come when we are growing up in our salvation. One of the key indicators of whether we are growing is whether we have that sense of the absolute goodness of the Lord, and are sensing His victory in our lives. John Maxwell has often said that people are either "winners" or "whiners." As followers of Jesus, we are most definitely winners who are headed to heaven. Meanwhile, we have received the life (*zoe*) that is truly life! Let us live that victory as we grow from infancy to childhood so others may want to experience it for themselves as well.

For the Questions For Discussion And Growth for
Craving Spiritual Milk go to page 28 now!

Questions For Discussion And Growth

Bios vs. *Zoe*

How does the distinction between *bios* and *zoe* help you see what Jesus meant when He said that we must be born again?

List several ways that "bios" and "zoe" differ:

    1)

    2)

    3)

List several ways that "bios" and "zoe" are similar:

    1)

    2)

    3)

What is the most significant aspect of "zoe" to you? Why?

The Walk Begins

How long were you an infant in the Lord, or are you still one? What do you do to ensure that growth happens in your life as a follower of Jesus?

What is one thing you need to do to see your growth accelerate and your maturity increase? When are you going to do it?

Learning To Lean On God (Proverbs 3:5-6)

What does it look like in your life when you trust God with all your heart and acknowledge Him in all your ways?

What costs have you paid for trusting God and not leaning on your own understanding?

What blessings have you received for trusting God and leaning on Him?

Moving Beyond Milk (Hebrews 5:11-14)

How does a person know he or she is moving on from spiritual milk to solid food according to Hebrews 5:11-14?

What is the sign of a mature believer according to this Scripture?

What are you doing to make certain that you move from spiritual milk to solid food?

Craving Spiritual Milk (1 Peter 2:1-3)

Why do you suppose Peter started out by listing aspects of evil that we must rid ourselves of in life before he told us to "crave the pure spiritual milk"?

What does it mean to you to "taste" and experience that the Lord is good?

What one thing did you take from 1 Peter 2:1-3 that will help you in growing to the next stage of development in your life as a follower of Jesus?

3

Childhood

[11]When I was a child, I spoke and thought and reasoned as a child.
But when I grew up, I put away childish things.

1 Corinthians 13:11 NLT

Introduction: Childlike vs. Childish

Sometimes words sound alike but have extremely different meanings. That is certainly the case with "childlike" and "childish." To be childlike is to be innocent, trusting, passionate and filled with joy and wonder just at being alive. To be childish is to throw tantrums, to demonstrate immaturity, to be self-centered and self-absorbed. Jesus showed us the vital nature of "childlikeness" in an exchange with His disciples found in Mark 10:13-16:

[13]One day some parents brought their children to Jesus so he could touch and bless them. But the disciples scolded the parents for bothering him.

[14]When Jesus saw what was happening, he was angry with his disciples. He said to them, "Let the children come to me. Don't stop them! For the Kingdom of God belongs to those who are like these children. [15]I tell you the truth, anyone who doesn't receive the Kingdom of God like a child will never enter it." [16]Then he took the children in his arms and placed his hands on their heads and blessed them. (Mark 10:13-16 NLT)

Wow! Unless we become "like a child" or "childlike" we will never enter the Kingdom of God. Being born again sets the life cycle of a Christian in motion. Growing through infancy is a necessary step to becoming a child. Being childlike is the next essential in the life cycle of a Christian. In this chapter, we examine four Scriptures that show us various elements of being children in Jesus Christ. We could select more, but these four show us what children who follow Jesus know; what children who follow Jesus are; how children who follow Jesus grow to maturity; and why we must move on from childhood as His followers. As you work your way through this chapter, pause often to reflect on whether your life has remained "childlike" or has simply been "childish." One of the paradoxical truths in the life cycle of a Christian is that in order to experience all the fullness Jesus has for us we **must** grow to maturity, while at the same time to experience all the fullness Jesus has for us we **must** remain childlike!

For the Questions For Discussion And Growth for Childlike vs. Childish go to page 39 now!

The Elementary Teachings (Hebrews 6:1-3)

One of the ways we distinguish between toddlers and children is that children go to school. In our day preschoolers may be as young as two or three, but we typically consider the start of formal schooling to be kindergarten, which starts for most children when they are five years old. In our Scripture from Hebrews 6:1-3, we are offered the six basic (elementary) teachings about Jesus. We find once again that the author of the Hebrews is somewhat less than patient as he urges his readers to stop going over the basics and to move on to more mature topics. For us, though, the reminder of the basic teachings about Jesus gives us the opportunity to see the content of the child phase of the life cycle of a Christian.

31

[1]So let us stop going over the basic teachings about Christ again and again. Let us go on instead and become mature in our understanding. Surely we don't need to start again with the fundamental importance of repenting from evil deeds and placing our faith in God. [2]You don't need further instruction about baptisms, the laying on of hands, the resurrection of the dead, and eternal judgment. [3]And so, God willing, we will move forward to further understanding. (Hebrews 6:1-3 NLT)

The six basic or elementary teachings of our faith are:

1) Repenting from evil deeds;
2) Placing our faith in God;
3) Baptisms;
4) The laying on of hands;
5) The resurrection of the dead; and
6) Eternal judgment.

You may have been surprised by what was and was not included in the elementary teachings of our faith. I was surprised to find the laying on of hands as an elementary teaching. Other than that, though, the six teachings cover the essential elements of life in Jesus Christ and maturing in Him. While it is beyond our scope to delve deeply into the six elementary teachings, here is a quick look at each one.

Repenting from evil deeds is the basic step in being born again. After all, in order to be born again, we must leave our old lives behind us. While the struggle between the old nature and the new one is ongoing, in order for us to move into a saving relationship with Jesus, we must acknowledge our evil deeds (our sins) and turn away from them (repent). Once we do that, we are ready to move on to the second elementary teaching.

Placing our faith in God is the essence of being born again. Jesus told us that being born again is a spiritual reality; and God is the source of all true spiritual reality. God—Father, Son and Holy

Spirit—is the object **and** the subject of our faith as God's children. Jesus' reminder that we must turn and become like children is instructive here. Children trust others by nature. Erik Eriksson said that the first two years of life are the period when an infant struggles with issues of "trust vs. mistrust." If the child's parents or caregivers are trustworthy, the child becomes trusting. We see evidence of such trust when a child leaps into a parent's arms from a set of steps or the back of sofa. In the same way, we take a leap of faith when we put our trust in God. Thankfully, He is always there to catch us!

The next elementary teaching may have caught you somewhat by surprise since it is *baptisms* plural instead of *baptism* singular. While we cannot say for sure exactly what the author meant, since we have only the one word to inform us, he must at least have meant baptism with water and baptism with the Holy Spirit. While some Christians believe the two are one and the same and others believe they are distinct events, the key for us here is that as children of God and followers of Jesus we are called to both baptisms. We are to be baptized in the name of the Father, the Son and the Holy Spirit as a response of faith (see Mark 16:16), which is a call to water baptism. We are to live our lives in the Spirit, which requires that we **must** be baptized in the Spirit (See Acts 1:5).

The laying on of hands is another of those acts carried out by followers of Jesus, which may have more than one meaning. It means at least this: In similar manner to the prophets of old, Jesus and the apostles laid hands on people in order to bless, confer ministry, cast out demons and bring about healing; thus, the church in every era is to pray and lay hands on others in similar situations.

The resurrection of the dead is perhaps the most elementary and basic of all Christian beliefs. As the Apostle Paul reminded the Corinthian believers, if Jesus has not been raised from the dead, then we are still dead in our sins and are of all people the most to be pitied (see 1 Corinthians 15). Jesus' resurrection demonstrated that He was not only the sacrificial "lamb" who died for the sins of the world but that He is, indeed, the Savior of the world. Just as His death was followed by resurrection, so we will one day be raised to eternal life when we die!

Eternal judgment is the final, elementary teaching of our faith. While many avoid, ignore or downplay the significance of the judgment to eternal life or eternal damnation, the teaching is common to all New Testament authors and, more importantly, to Jesus in His teaching as well. Therefore, we must make certain it is part of our teaching and learning.

As we seek to grow in our faith, moving from birth to infancy to childhood, these elementary teachings lay the groundwork for our life in Jesus and lead us into deeper matters of our faith.

For the Questions For Discussion And Growth for
Elementary Teachings go to page 40 now!

The Spirit of Adoption (Romans 8:12-17)

While all Scripture is inspired by God and is, therefore, true, there is no greater truth in all of God's word than this one: *We, who were once dead in sin and destined for eternal death as a result, can become "children of God."* This transformation cannot be earned, bought or calculated with our minds. This transformation is a gift from God. Just as human parents adopt a child for the child's benefit, without cost to the child; so God our Heavenly Father adopts us and makes us His spiritual children at no cost to us—but at the greatest of all costs to His only natural son, Jesus! The Apostle Paul explains this amazing reality:

[12]Therefore, dear brothers and sisters, you have no obligation to do what your sinful nature urges you to do. [13]For if you live by its dictates, you will die. But if

through the power of the Spirit you put to death the deeds of your sinful nature, you will live. [14]For all who are led by the Spirit of God are children of God. [15]So you have not received a spirit that makes you fearful slaves. Instead, you received God's Spirit when he adopted you as his own children. Now we call him, "Abba, Father." [16]For his Spirit joins with our spirit to affirm that we are God's children. [17]And since we are his children, we are his heirs. In fact, together with Christ we are heirs of God's glory. But if we are to share his glory, we must also share his suffering. (Romans 8:12-17 NLT)

In the middle of this amazing Scripture, Paul tells us that because we are adopted by God, we may cry out to Him, "Abba, Father!" A more literal translation would be, "Abba, Daddy!" Abba is the Aramaic word used by toddlers and children for their fathers. The English equivalent is "Daddy." How incredible is that! We may call the God of the universe Daddy because of what He has done for us in Jesus Christ. Paul makes it clear that we had nothing to do with this. This is God's doing completely. In fact, he tells us if we continue to live according to the dictates of our sinful nature we will die. He is not talking only of physical death but also of spiritual death. It is "dying twice." We must live through the power of the Holy Spirit. As we give the Holy Spirit power and authority in our lives, He puts to death the deeds of the sinful nature in our lives; and we truly live.

The key we must recognize in this Scripture is that we are sinful by birth and destined for death, but Jesus intercedes for us. Jesus makes us God's children. If we are ever to mature from the new birth, through infancy to childhood, it will be because of Jesus' blood poured out on the cross to cancel our sins and give us new life. Then His Holy Spirit lives in us to bring us to maturity. Once again, being God's children as we are using the word here is something we will remain **forever**. While Jesus plans for us to continue to grow into "adulthood," we will always remain His "child." Anyone who is a parent (or an adult child with parents who are still living) understands this reality. While Abby, our older daughter is an adult, she still calls me "Daddy;" and from my perspective she will always be my child. If we ever find ourselves doubting God's love or presence in our lives, we need look no farther than Romans 8:12-17 to remind us that God loves us so much that He has adopted us into His eternal family. As a result, we are His children, His "heirs" and co-heirs with Jesus of God's Glory!

For the Questions For Discussion And Growth for
The Spirit Of Adoption go to page 41 now!

Renewed Minds (Romans 12:1-2)

Many times, I have heard people say that in order to be a Christian a person has to "check his mind at the door." Nothing could be farther from the truth. In fact, as Romans 12:1-2 makes clear growth in our walk with God comes by the "renewing of our minds." Let us look at this important teaching from the Apostle Paul:

> [1]Therefore, I urge you, brothers, in view of God's mercy, to offer your bodies as living sacrifices, holy and pleasing to God—this is your spiritual act of worship. [2]Do not conform any longer to the pattern of this world, but be transformed by the renewing of your mind. Then you will be able to test and approve what God's will is—his good, pleasing and perfect will. (Romans 12:12 NIV)

Paul reminds us that as a response to God's mercy in our lives—the mercy which opens the door for our adoption as His sons and daughters—we are called to offer our lives to Him. Paul tells us to be "living sacrifices." It has been said that the problem with living sacrifices is they tend to "crawl off the altar." We do! We want to follow God. We want to grow up in Him. We want to move through the life cycle of a Christian, but we tend to stall at many points along the way. We find the going tough, so we slow down or take a break. We experience trials and temptations, and we assume that no one has ever gone through what we are going through in the history of humanity. The reality is our trials and temptations are well known to Jesus. He went through them, too. The difference is He came through them without sin. That is why He alone can offer us new life.

Once we are reborn, we have the challenge of growing. How do we do that? We do it in a way that surprises many people because it involves the **mind**! Look again at what Paul wrote, "[2]Do not conform any longer to the pattern of this world, but be transformed by the renewing of your mind." The world seeks to mold us into its shape or pattern. We are bombarded day after day with messages telling us to "look out for number one," "indulge yourself," "you **deserve** the best;" and we buy it—for a time. We get caught up in climbing the ladder of success, being the most popular person at school or attaining the highest grades or the best win-loss record. Before we know it, the world's ways have become such a natural part of us that growing up in Jesus Christ sounds impossible. Paul tells us we cannot conform to this world **and** be transformed into the image of Jesus. Something has to give! We must exchange the mindset of the world for a new mindset—the mindset of Jesus Christ. The world says, "Take!" Jesus says, "Give!" The world says, "Mine!" Jesus says, "I have given all for you!" In order to grow up into Jesus' likeness we must exchange the world's thoughts for Jesus' thoughts. Much is made of worldview these days, as it must be. We cannot grow into a fully developing follower of Jesus if we hold onto a worldview that reflects the world! We must develop a biblical worldview in order to grow into a spiritually mature adult. Remember, *the life in Jesus Christ means* *learning in order to grow more like Jesus.* It means becoming all that God created us to be, because when we are most fully the one God created us to be; we will most fully reflect Jesus! After all, God created each of us in His own image. When the sin that has broken and tarnished that image is overcome by the renewing of our minds, we look like Him once again. We will never become "gods," as some religions and worldviews proclaim. We will reflect the image of God as our minds become more and more renewed in Him. As the moon reflects the sun, so our lives reflect Jesus.

For the Questions For Discussion And Growth for
Renewed Minds go to page 41 now!

Moving on From Childhood (1 Corinthians 13:11)

As we close out this chapter on childhood, we turn once again to the Apostle Paul to tell us why we must mature in order to be all Jesus calls us to be. While 1 Corinthians 13 is often referred to as "the love chapter" for its well-known beginning verses, 1 Corinthians 13:11 reminds us that we were never intended to remain children. We are called to grow up: "[11]When I was a child, I spoke and thought and reasoned as a child. But when I grew up, I put away childish things." (1 Corinthians 13:11 NLT).

Simple enough, isn't it? As children, we speak, think and reason as children. Childlike reasoning and even childish reasoning are cute—for children. However, when we grow up physically but not spiritually, the result is something none of us wants in our lives. The time comes for each of us to put away childish things. From my perspective, *children are being rushed through biological childhood too fast yet through spiritual childhood too slowly.* Parents pressure children to attain the highest possible grades in elementary school lest they miss the opportunity to get into the "best" colleges and universities. Children are pressured to perform like adults on sports fields across America. (That statement hits a little too close to home for me; I have been one of those parent-coaches who at times has been more concerned with developing the best players and teams and not as concerned with enjoying the fun of participation.) On the other hand, children are not challenged to grow up in the area that really matters—spiritually. It should come as no surprise that our children go off to college ill-equipped to defend a biblical worldview and choose to adopt alternatives offered by professors who seem so much more intelligent and well equipped to defend theirs. The Apostle Paul rightly reminds us that the time comes in each of our lives to put childish things behind us so we can pursue the matters of eternity! If we do not put those childish ways behind us, one day we may find ourselves adopting a worldview that holds no promise or certainty for eternity, because only Jesus offers that.

For the Questions For Discussion And Growth for
Moving On From Childhood go to page 42 now!

Questions For Discussion And Growth

Childlike vs. Childish

In addition to the distinctions made in the introduction between childlikeness and childishness, what distinctions come to mind for you?

Why do you suppose the disciples did not think it was worth bothering Jesus to bring children to Him to bless them?

What is the most important thing you learn from Mark 10:13-16? What are the implications from it for how you will live each day?

Elementary Teachings (Hebrews 6:1-3)

Which of the six elementary teachings of our faith most surprised you? Why?

Is there another teaching of our faith that you find as more basic or elementary than these? If so, what is it?

How does living out these six basic teachings identify us as children of God?

The Spirit Of Adoption (Romans 8:12-17)

What does it mean to you that you are "adopted" as a child of God?

What is the most significant truth in Romans 8:12-17 for you?

What is one action you need to take as a result of reading Romans 8:12-17?

Renewed Minds (Romans 12:1-2)

What does it mean to you to be a "living sacrifice"?

How do you make certain that you are not "conformed" (or molded) to this world?

What does it look like in daily life when you are being "transformed by the renewing of your mind"?

Moving on From Childhood (1 Corinthians 13:11)

Do you agree or disagree with the statement that too much emphasis is placed on growing up biologically and too little on growing spiritually? Why?

In what ways have you moved away from childish things in your spiritual growth?

What does it look like in your daily life when you are actually living 1 Corinthians 13:11?

4

Discipleship

*11*I have hidden your word in my heart,
that I might not sin against you. (Psalm 119:11 NLT)

Introduction: Picking up the Yoke of Jesus

We take a turn now in our focus as we leave childhood and move to spiritual adolescence and adulthood. Chapters four through seven emphasize the major components of maturing as followers of Jesus. These components are life-long undertakings. We never grow beyond our need for discipleship, living in the Spirit, encouraging one another, holding one another accountable and mentoring and being mentored. The most exciting truth of this maturing process is Jesus always comes alongside us as we move forward. Jesus recognized that living the *bios* life, pursuing the world's version of success, is ultimately futile, so He offers us something more. As you read His words below, imagine Him speaking them directly to you—because He is!

[28]Then Jesus said, "Come to me, all of you who are weary and carry heavy burdens, and I will give you rest. [29]Take my yoke upon you. Let me teach you, because I am humble and gentle at heart, and you will find rest for your souls. [30]For my yoke is easy to bear, and the burden I give you is light. (Matthew 11:28-20 NLT).

The beginning of discipleship, of moving beyond childhood and into true maturity as Jesus' followers, is picking up His yoke. You may or may not be acquainted with that term. In Jesus' day (and in many places today) a yoke was an instrument used to connect two animals, usually oxen, to one another so they could pull a plow or a cart. When Jesus told us we may take His yoke upon ourselves, when we are weary and our burdens seem too heavy, He was offering to shoulder our load with us. Jesus wants us to bind ourselves to Him, so we may work together in this process of becoming like Him! Notice that Jesus tells us he will not drag us or abuse us along the way. He is "humble and gentle at heart." Putting His yoke on our lives means rest for our souls. What an offer! Jesus' yoke is easy and the burden He gives us is light. The world's yoke is always hard and heavy because it is based on performance. I have spoken with many folks who are about my age (fifty-one at the time of this writing) and have heard this recurring theme: "I just can't do what I used to do." As we age physically, our ability to complete tasks wanes, especially physical tasks. Jesus tells us He will not over burden us when we yoke ourselves to Him. Indeed, one of the blessings I am experiencing as my physical capacities diminish little by little (and sometimes not so little by little!) is I have never been stronger in Jesus! His presence by the Holy Spirit is more real than ever. The strength to do His will grows day by day. As we consider what it means to be His disciples, to grow throughout the life cycle of a Christian, how amazing it is that the Lord of the universe takes our burdens upon Himself! As our ability to carry it diminishes, He bears all the more. Discipleship does not gain us greater favor with Jesus. Whether we protect ourselves from evil, memorize scripture, listen carefully to Jesus' voice, worship with our brothers and sisters, pray and yield more and more control to Him—or not—His love is constant. However, as we do protect ourselves from evil, memorize scripture, listen carefully to Jesus' voice, worship with our brothers and sisters, pray and yield more and more control to Him, our lives become more and more like His. Jesus' yoke becomes a natural part of our daily "attire," and our lives gain a significance and joy that cannot be found in any other pursuit or relationship. May each of us lay our burdens on Jesus' shoulders and pick up His yoke. As we do, we can be sure that our lives will take a literal turn in the right direction—since that is always the direction Jesus leads.

For the Questions For Discussion And Growth for *Introduction: Picking Up The Yoke Of Jesus* go to page 53 now!

Guard Your Heart (Proverbs 4:23)

In order to become a disciple of Jesus, an intentional step of growth in the life cycle of a Christian, we must start to fill our hearts with Jesus' truth and the truth of the entire Bible. In his excellent book, *Change Your Heart, Change Your Life,* Gary Smalley goes into minute detail about how this process takes place. To summarize it here, the process of heart change means taking beliefs that have become ingrained in our hearts through thousands of repetitions in our lives and replacing them with truth from God's word. For example, in my formative years, the role model I had for responding to undesired situations "defaulted" to anger. My dad had a volatile temper and when things did not go well, everyone experienced his displeasure. After watching that repeatedly from infancy onward, I developed a belief—it was an incorrect belief, but it was my belief nevertheless. I believed that when things did not go my way, the appropriate response was anger. That belief became ingrained in my heart. What I learned from reading *Change Your Heart, Change Your Life* is God can (and does) change the beliefs of our hearts when we yield them to Him and replace them with His truth. In my case, I have been memorizing or focusing on Scriptures to help me dislodge the errant belief that anger is the appropriate response when life does not go my way. The most helpful Scripture for me has been one I have known since childhood: "[12]So in everything, do to others what you would have them do to you, for this sums up the Law and the Prophets" (Matthew 7:12 NIV). We call it the Golden Rule. As I have repeated that truth over and over, I am finding that God is using it to change my heart, my belief and my response to situations that used to produce anger automatically. After all, no one I know enjoys having someone respond with anger when something goes wrong. The process Gary Smalley describes so effectively has been around for a long time. Three thousand years ago, King Solomon put it this way: "[23]Above all else, guard your heart, for it is the wellspring of life" (Proverbs 4:23 NIV).

Since we want to grow to be more like Jesus, we must guard our hearts. The goal of discipleship is to become fully mature. The Apostle Paul called it growing up into the full stature of Jesus Christ. With that as our goal, the starting point is placing the truth of God's Word in our hearts and then **guarding** that truth with our lives. That may sound a bit extreme, but think about it: What is more important to someone who wants to be like Jesus, than making certain that the beliefs of our hearts are based in His life and teaching? The world offers us so many opportunities to fill our hearts with garbage. I am not advocating that we become hermits, that we separate ourselves from the world. I am advocating that we fill our hearts with Jesus' examples and teachings so that when the world offers us false beliefs, ideas and examples we will recognize them for what they are and reject them.

When our children are small, we, as parents, protect them and guard them from harm. As they grow, we teach them to protect and guard themselves. If that is true in the physical realm—and it is—how much more true it is in matters of the heart! To stay with our analogy for a moment, when our children start to take responsibility for guarding and protecting their own lives, they move on from childhood to maturity. In the same way, when we take responsibility for guarding our hearts, we move on from spiritual childhood and into adolescence and, ultimately, adulthood.

For the Questions For Discussion And Growth for
Guard Your Heart go to page 54 now!

Hiding God's Word in Our Hearts (Psalm 119:11)

Every consideration of growing as Jesus' disciples must include reading and studying God's word. Many helpful books have been written on this topic. One of my favorites is *Rick Warren's Bible Study Methods: Twelve Ways You Can Unlock God's Word.* If we are going to guard our hearts by filling them with God's word, then we must read, study, remember and live out God's word! One of the best Scriptures for helping us see the relationship between God's word and the transformation of our lives is Psalm 119:11: "[11]I have hidden your word in my heart that I might not sin against you." (NIV).

When we hide, that is when we store, imprint, repeat, digest and enact God's word, so it becomes part of our hearts we equip ourselves to overcome sin. Memorizing God's word does not guarantee we will not sin, but it makes certain that we know what God expects of us and what it means to live in righteousness. If we go back to Jesus' words about picking up His yoke and connecting ourselves to Him, God's word is part of the yoke. The teachings themselves connect us to Jesus. Jesus reminded His followers that He did not come to destroy the "Law and the Prophets" (much of what we call the Old Testament). He came to fulfill them. As His followers, who seek to grow up into the full stature of Jesus, we must read and study God's word, "hiding" it in our hearts. Then when we face a test, trial or temptation, we can call on that truth to instruct and guide us through it.

One of the most important examples Jesus offered us of the importance of learning God's word as part of our maturational process came when He faced severe temptation in the wilderness at the beginning of His earthly ministry. He had fasted for forty days after His baptism. In that state of hunger and general physical weakness, He faced three temptations from the devil. In reading the account in Matthew 4, we find that in response to each temptation Jesus quoted God's word. Jesus' example reminds us that to be ready for any kind of temptation—and we **will** face temptation as Jesus' followers—we must hide God's word in our hearts. Then we will be armed to overcome it as He did!

For the Questions For Discussion And Growth for *Hiding God's Word In Our Hearts* go to page 55 now!

Hearing God's Voice (John 10:1-5)

Another challenge we face in growing as Jesus' followers is to hear His voice as we go through daily life. I have heard many people say, "God told me to _____," (the blank may be filled with any number of actions: go visit my mother, write a letter to the editor, speak up at a public meeting where God's perspective is not being presented, leave my wife, rest, etc…). How do we know God is speaking to us in such situations and that it is not just our own voice? One of the most helpful books on hearing God and knowing His will is Henry Blackaby's *Experiencing God.* (If you are noticing a trend here, good job! I am offering you the opportunity to develop a discipleship library by citing helpful works in the various areas of discipleship we are considering. For the list, see the Appendix.) Blackaby states that God speaks to us most clearly through the Bible.

After all, the Bible **is** God's word. He also speaks to us through prayer, circumstances and other believers. When He speaks to us through other believers, circumstances or prayer, we must **always** examine what we hear against His written word. God never contradicts His own word when He speaks to us by other means. Jesus told folks how He speaks to us by using an agricultural analogy. Here is how He put it:

> [1]"I tell you the truth, the man who does not enter the sheep pen by the gate, but climbs in by some other way, is a thief and a robber. [2]The man who enters by the gate is the shepherd of his sheep. [3]The watchman opens the gate for him, and the sheep listen to his voice. He calls his own sheep by name and leads them out. [4]When he has brought out all his own, he goes on ahead of them, and his sheep follow him because they know his voice. [5]But they will never follow a stranger; in fact, they will run away from him because they do not recognize a stranger's voice." (John 10:1-5 NIV)

Jesus teaches us many things here, but the most important may be this: *Jesus **does** call us when we belong to Him.* Sometimes we feel Jesus has forgotten us because He seems to be silent. Jesus told us that He **calls** His sheep—He calls us! He also said we will **listen** to his voice, and we will not follow a stranger. What a helpful promise! The question for us becomes, "Am I Jesus' 'sheep'?" Since you have made it this far with me, you know you **are** His "sheep" if you have been born again. So, as Jesus' sheep, we have the ability to hear and discern His voice from the voice of strangers. That ability grows as we grow in Him. When we intentionally follow and obey Jesus, our ability to listen and discern grows. Every time we say Yes to Jesus and do what He calls us to do, we get better at hearing and discerning His voice. The challenge we face is to keep our ears inclined to Jesus in the midst of the chaos that surrounds us. Growing disciples know that the only way to navigate through all the obstacles life sets before us, is to listen and live according to the Shepherd's voice!

For the Questions For Discussion And Growth for
Hearing God's Voice go to page 56 now!

When You Pray (Matthew 6:5-13)

You may be wondering, "Isn't Hearing God's voice part of prayer?" Yes! It most definitely is. In fact, because it is the most important aspect of prayer, I addressed it under a separate heading. Now, we address what most people think of when they hear the word *prayer*—talking to God. When we talk to God, we must remember that prayer includes His response to us as well! So often, we run to God with our needs, wants and problems. We cry out to Him for help. Then, we run off to take care of our needs, wants and problems **on our own**. As disciples of Jesus, we must learn to listen after we have spoken—and sometimes before we speak—to God! Jesus offered a clear teaching on prayer in His Sermon on the Mount:

[5]"And when you pray, do not be like the hypocrites, for they love to pray standing in the synagogues and on the street corners to be seen by men. I tell you the truth, they have received their reward in full. [6]But when you pray, go into your room, close the door and pray to your Father, who is unseen. Then your Father, who sees what is done in secret, will reward you. [7]And when you pray, do not keep on babbling like pagans, for they think they will be heard because of their many words. [8]Do not be like them, for your Father knows what you need before you ask him. [9]"This, then, is how you should pray:

"'Our Father in heaven, hallowed be your name, [10]your kingdom come, your will be done on earth as it is in heaven. [11]Give us today our daily bread. [12]Forgive us our debts, as we also have forgiven our debtors. [13]And lead us not into temptation, but deliver us from the evil one.' (Matthew 6:5-13 NIV)

50

Jesus' instructions on prayer come in three, distinct parts. First, we are not to be like hypocrites when we pray, that is, we must not pray for "show." When we pray in worship, in a small group or in public, our prayers are not for the benefit of those around us to hear. They are especially not a means of making others think more highly of us. Prayer is always directed to God. Jesus tells us when we pray for public acclaim all we get is public acclaim. However, when we pray privately, when we get together just with God, He hears our prayers and rewards us. That is a great promise, don't you think?

Next, Jesus tells us when we pray we are not to babble on like pagans who think God is bound to answer a prayer, just because they pray long enough, hard enough, loud enough or with the right words. God is not bound to answer our prayers based on anything we do. *God's response to our prayers is based on one reality: God loves us more than we love ourselves.* God desires to abide with us (that is, to remain and connect with us), and He is more loving than any earthly parent could ever be. He always gives us what we need—not necessarily what we want, but what we need.

Finally, Jesus offers what we usually call the Lord's Prayer. It could just as easily be called the Disciples' Prayer since Jesus gave it to His disciples to show us how to pray. The prayer calls us to praise God and to remember we have an intimate relationship with Him. He even invites us to call God "Father." The prayer calls us to ask for God's will to be done here on earth as it is already done in heaven. (Think about that. Far from telling us to pray for God to "take us home" to heaven, Jesus calls us to pray for God to bring heaven **here!** That makes our daily lives incredibly significant. Since we are citizens of heaven already, we have the opportunity to show others how they can become citizens of heaven as well.) Next, Jesus reminds us to ask God to provide our daily needs because nothing is too small for us to take to God in prayer. Then He reminds us to call on God for forgiveness and to ask for the power to forgive others. After all, if we receive forgiveness only as we forgive others, we need to ask God to give us the power to forgive others, since that power does not come naturally. Finally, Jesus tells us to call on God to keep us away from temptation and, in those times when we find ourselves there anyway, to deliver us from its source—the "evil one"—Satan. This prayer shows growing disciples how to invest our time in prayer. As we close this section on prayer, remember that our agenda is only one part of prayer. The most important part is God's response, so when you pray be sure to LISTEN as well as speak!

For the Questions For Discussion And Growth for
When You Pray go to page 57 now!

Which God Will Rule Your Heart? (Matthew 6:19-21)

As we close our consideration of discipleship, we move to another matter of the heart. This time, we look at who rules our hearts. Jesus taught that our hearts can only have one master, one ruler:

> [Jesus said] [19]"Do not store up for yourselves treasures on earth, where moth and rust destroy, and where thieves break in and steal. [20]But store up for yourselves treasures in heaven, where moth and rust do not destroy, and where thieves do not break in and steal. [21]For where your treasure is, there your heart will be also. (Matthew 6:19-21 NIV)

Later in this passage Jesus said, "You cannot serve both God and money." (Matthew 6:24) As followers of Jesus, our growth is dependent on giving our absolute allegiance to Him. If we devote our lives to the accumulation of wealth, we have chosen an alternate ruler. If we do that, at best we will stagnate in our growth as Jesus' followers. At worst, we will turn from Jesus and lose the joy that comes from serving Him. Jesus points out the transitory nature of earthly treasure: It rusts, crumbles and gets lost and stolen. If we invest our lives in pursuing such things, our hearts eventually change in ways we live to regret. Some invest their whole lives in worldly treasure. Some go to their graves thinking they made the right decision. Yet, in the instant they pass from this life to the next, and face Jesus, they discover that only the heart devoted to Him is granted entrance to heaven. By then it is too late.

I once met a man who was a few days from death. A friend of his had asked me if I would go and talk to the man about Jesus. I jumped at the opportunity! As we talked, the man's heart softened and although he had invested his entire adult life in pursuing worldly treasure, he yielded his heart to Jesus. He said something I have always remembered: "I have invested my whole life in the wrong thing." Thank God that he did not invest his **whole** life in the wrong thing. In the last few days, he came to understand what really mattered—Jesus. What amazing grace God offers that our allegiances may change—our hearts may be offered to Him—right up to the last breath of life! Far better is the heart devoted to Jesus early. Double blessing comes for that heart because it enjoys fellowship with Jesus **now**—and in the life to come!

For the Questions For Discussion And Growth for
Which God Will Rule Your Heart go to page 57 now!

Questions For Discussion And Growth

Introduction: Picking Up The Yoke Of Jesus

Why do you think Jesus used the image of yoking ourselves to Him in order to ease our burdens in life?

What burdens do you need to hand over to Jesus right now in order to receive His "lighter load"?

What is the most important application of this Scripture for you?

Guard Your Heart (Proverbs 4:23)

What incorrect beliefs have become anchored in your heart and need to be replaced by the truth of God's word?

What specific steps do you take to guard your heart?

Based on the steps you are currently taking to guard your heart, where are you in the process of growth (e.g., infant, child, adolescent or adult)? What do you need to do to move to the next stage?

Hiding God's Word In Our Hearts (Psalm 119:11)

What are you doing to hide God's word in your heart on a regular basis?

When you face temptations, do you find that God's word comes to mind to give you the power to overcome it? If not, what could you do to encourage that?

What does the amount of time and energy you put into studying God's word say about your growth in Jesus right now? What do you want it to say?

Hearing God's Voice (John 10:1-5)

How do you respond to Henry Blackaby's statement that God speaks most clearly to us through the Bible?

Has God ever spoken to you through prayer, circumstances or other believers? If so, give an example.

When has Jesus spoken to you recently? What have you done about what He said?

What do you need to do right now to hear Jesus' voice more clearly?

When You Pray (Matthew 6:5-13)

Do you ever pray aloud in public? If so, how do you ensure that it isn't just for show?

Have you ever repeated a prayer over and over again, thinking that it would cause God to answer? If so, what was the situation?

What aspect of the Lord's Prayer is the most challenging for you? Why?

Which God Will Rule Your Heart (Matthew 6:19-21)

What does it mean to you to have Jesus ruling your heart?

Why do you think God offers entrance to heaven even to those who do not give Him their hearts until they are on their deathbeds?

What do you need to do right now to yield more of your heart to Jesus?

5

Life in the Spirit

"[Jesus said,] ^{5}For John baptized with water, but in a few days you
will be baptized with the Holy Spirit." (Acts 1:5 NIV)

Introduction: Jesus' Presence in Daily Life

If this book ended in chapter four, it would be like a flashlight
without batteries. In fact, while discipleship calls us to live like Jesus,
to grow up into maturity and to reflect the full stature of Jesus in our
lives, we cannot be or become disciples in our own power. As you
read the Gospel accounts in the New Testament, what appears
obvious is that Jesus' disciples often failed to think, speak or act like
Him. They fell short in **every** area. Yet, after Jesus died, rose again,
ascended into heaven and sent the Holy Spirit on the first Christian
Pentecost, the disciples were transformed. Jesus literally became
present in their lives. Instead of trying or even training to be like
Jesus, they let Jesus live in them and their lives became like His. As
we will discuss in the final chapter, Jesus' followers eventually told
others to imitate them as they imitated Him. Their lives became so
filled with His life through the Holy Spirit that the Apostle Paul said,
"It is no longer I who live, but Christ lives in me" (Galatians 2:20b
NLT).

As we consider what it means to live life in the Spirit, understand
that Christians of good character disagree about the scope and extent
of the Holy Spirit's presence and activity in our lives today. Some

contend that the obvious work of the Holy Spirit ended at the close of the Apostolic Age (when the last of Jesus' apostles died). Others contend the Holy Spirit's active, visible work is only for areas where Jesus has not yet been preached, which would be why miracles occur among primitive tribes and peoples but not in the "developed" world. As I read Scripture, the Holy Spirit is still active and engaged in our daily lives wherever we are. A life of discipleship devoid of the Spirit's power is futile. If one "succeeds" he or she becomes pharisaical because the effort is one's own. More likely one "fails" in the endeavor, becomes frustrated and either gives up or makes excuses for the failure. Jesus' demands on those who follow Him are so radical that only His vital presence in us by the Holy Spirit offers hope of living them out in daily life. But, the good news is—the Holy Spirit **is** available to empower us to live them! As my good friend, John Nuzzo says, "When you consider the work of the Holy Spirit as presented in the New Testament, you have only three responses: 1) The message is not true. 2) The message is true and I want that in my life. Or 3) I need more information." It is beyond the scope of this book to delve deeply into the life in the Spirit. The goal here is to make clear that Jesus' presence in our daily life **is** available to all who follow Him through the ongoing work of the Holy Spirit.

For the Questions For Discussion And Growth for
Introduction: Jesus' Presence In Daily Life go to page 68 now!

The Promise of the Holy Spirit (Acts 1:3b-5)

In order to establish that the Holy Spirit IS available to us in our daily lives, we turn to Jesus' words to His original followers in Acts 1:3b-5. As the text tells us, Jesus appeared to His followers over a forty-day period after His resurrection from the dead. In the appearance described below Jesus promised that the Holy Spirit would come:

> He [Jesus] appeared to them over a period of forty days and spoke about the kingdom of God. ⁴On one occasion, while he was eating with them, he gave them this command: "Do not leave Jerusalem, but wait for the gift my Father promised, which you have heard me speak about. ⁵For John baptized with water, but in a few days you will be baptized with the Holy Spirit." (Acts 1:3b-5 NIV)

The gift Jesus' Father had promised was the Holy Spirit. Luke 24:49 makes that clear, as well as Jesus' statement in Acts 1:5. Jesus made a distinction between John's baptism, which was with water, and His baptism, which would be with the Holy Spirit. John had said the same thing during his ministry of preparation for Jesus' coming into the world. John said,

> ¹¹"I baptize with water those who repent of their sins and turn to God. But someone is coming soon who is greater than I am—so much greater that I'm not worthy even to be his slave and carry his sandals. He will baptize you with the Holy Spirit and with fire. (Matthew 3:11 NLT)

The promised Holy Spirit had not yet come to the disciples, but Jesus said the Spirit would come and they would be baptized in (or with Him) in a few days. The promised coming of the Holy Spirit occurred ten days later on the first Christian Pentecost. As Acts 2 describes it, the coming of the Holy Spirit was a dramatic event. Those who received the Holy Spirit spoke in tongues (languages they had never learned), and those they told responded by the thousands to God's Good News of redemption through Jesus. Even though we live nearly 2,000 years **after** the fulfillment of the promise, we can be sure the promise is still ours. The Apostle Peter told us so in Acts 2:38-39.

> ³⁸Peter replied, "Each of you must repent of your sins and turn to God, and be baptized in the name of Jesus Christ to show that you have received forgiveness for your sins. Then

you will receive the gift of the Holy Spirit. [39]This promise is to you, and to your children, and even to the Gentiles—all who have been called by the Lord our God." (Acts 2:38-39 NLT)

"This promise" is surely the promise of the Holy Spirit. It was not only for those who stood and listened to Peter on that day so long ago but also to their children and the Gentiles—to all who have been called by the Lord our God—including us!

For the Questions For Discussion And Growth for
The Promise Of The Holy Spirit go to page 69 now!

Wait, Receive Power, Go! (Acts 1:8)

After promising the disciples they would receive the Holy Spirit in a few days, Jesus gave them one final instruction before returning to heaven. That instruction forms the basis for all evangelism in Jesus' name:

> [7]He said to them: "It is not for you to know the times or dates the Father has set by his own authority. [8]But you will receive power when the Holy Spirit comes on you; and you will be my witnesses in Jerusalem, and in all Judea and Samaria, and to the ends of the earth." (Acts 1:7-8 NIV)

Jesus' words may be broken down into three simple commands: Wait. Receive Power. Go. We must keep the commands in that order. First, we wait. We wait until the Holy Spirit comes. When we act without the Holy Spirit's presence, the best we can hope for is humanistic altruism. The best we can hope for is disciples who follow us, not Jesus. We must not act until we have received the Holy Spirit. The disciples waited for ten days before the Holy Spirit came. One wonders whether any group of believers in our day would wait for ten days before doing something! Many times Jesus' followers are so eager to act, to "take the next hill," that we forget Jesus' first command when it comes to serving Him: **wait**.

We wait until we receive power. The power source for all we are and do as Jesus' followers is the Holy Spirit. The disciples waited and prayed for ten days. Finally, the Holy Spirit came. Then they received the power Jesus had promised. The power went beyond any natural power in the world. When we think of power, we often think of force, wealth or status. Jesus' use of the word power goes beyond any of those definitions. The power of the Holy Spirit is the power of God to transform human lives. That power brings love where there was once hate or apathy. It brings joy where there was once merely happiness or despair. The power of the Holy Spirit is the power to see the earthly become eternal.

Once we have received that power, Jesus tells us to go. The moment the Holy Spirit came into the lives of those original followers of Jesus they ran from the house where they had been waiting and praying and into the streets to tell everyone about Jesus. The power of the Holy Spirit always comes to us, so we may pass it on to others. The Good News of salvation is not ours to own, but to offer to everyone. Jesus gave His followers an intentional plan for their going. He told them to be His witnesses in Jerusalem (where they were), all Judea and Samaria (their native land and the country next-door) and to the ends of the earth. Some contend the instruction meant the disciples were to stay in Jerusalem until **all** in Jerusalem had heard the Good News. The remainder of the Book of Acts tells us that Jesus' intention was for the disciples to go into all of the areas mentioned progressively and concurrently. They were to start in Jerusalem and spread out while Jerusalem was being reached.

Jesus' simple instructions are so powerful for us who follow Him today. We must tell others about Jesus; but **before** we do that, we must wait until we receive power. Balancing the waiting and the going with receiving power is crucial. So many times we miss it either by our eagerness to go or our hesitancy to do anything because we are not sure whether the power has come. Remember the flashlight analogy? Without batteries, a flashlight is just a collection of useless parts; but with batteries, a flashlight illuminates the dark! Wait. Receive power! (Insert batteries!) Go! (Illuminate the darkness!)

For the Questions For Discussion And Growth for
Wait. Receive Power. Go. go to page 70 now!

Be Filled... (Ephesians 5:15-21)

No verse concerning the Holy Spirit may be overlooked more often than Ephesians 5:18: "Don't be drunk with wine, because that will ruin your life. Instead, be filled with the Holy Spirit" (NLT). This brief verse shows us how to live life in the Spirit every day. Here it is in its context:

> [15]So be careful how you live. Don't live like fools, but like those who are wise. [16]Make the most of every opportunity in these evil days. [17]Don't act thoughtlessly, but understand what the Lord wants you to do. **[18]Don't be drunk with wine, because that will ruin your life.** Instead, be filled with the Holy Spirit, [19]singing psalms and hymns and spiritual songs among yourselves, and making music to the Lord in your hearts. [20]And give thanks for everything to God the Father in the name of our Lord Jesus Christ. [21]And further, submit to one another out of reverence for Christ. (Ephesians 5:15-21 NLT)

The Apostle Paul tells us we must be careful (intentional) in living our lives as followers of Jesus. Why? The times are evil. Many deny the existence of evil, but it does not take a rocket scientist to see the extent of evil reported daily on the news. More heinous and senseless crimes are committed each day. Paul tells us in the midst of such times, we must live as those who are wise, to understand what the

Lord wants us to do. The question is **how** we do that? How do we become wise? How do we understand what the Lord wants us to do? Verse 18 tells us. First, we are told what **not** to do, which is helpful, since we can learn both by avoiding the negative and engaging the positive in life. What we are **not** supposed to do is get drunk with wine. Why? It will ruin our lives. Addictions ruin countless lives. Alcohol and other drugs destroy not only those who abuse them but also relatives, friends, coworkers and even strangers. No one intends to become an alcoholic or a drug addict; but the Apostle Paul reminds us if we do not get drunk, we will avoid the long-term consequences of ruined lives.

Next Paul tells us what we **are** supposed to do: "Be filled with the Holy Spirit." The statement is so simple. In our English translations it is not as clear as it needs to be. The verb Paul used in the original Greek was a present, passive, imperative. That means the action is **continuous**. It does not mean for us to be filled with the Holy Spirit **once** and that will take care of it for the rest of our lives. It means **be being** filled with the Holy Spirit. Be filled moment-by-moment, day-by-day. That is so vital! If we are to live out Jesus' commands in our lives, we need a power source greater than ourselves or we will surely fail. We need the Holy Spirit. We do not need a "dose" of the Holy Spirit; we need His on-going presence filling and empowering us. The verb being in the passive voice means we cannot do it in our own power. Paul did not tell us "Fill yourselves up with the Holy Spirit," as if we could do that. He told us to "be filled" with the Holy Spirit. In other words, we must open ourselves to the Holy Spirit and let Him fill us up. A great analogy for explaining this is to consider ourselves as "empty bottles" with "lids". The only thing we can do to be "filled" is to take off the "lid", and "open" ourselves to being filled with the Holy Spirit. As we do that, the Holy Spirit fills us. In that moment we are empowered to experience the transformation Jesus gave His life for us to know. Finally, the verb is an imperative—a

65

command. We **must** be filled with the Holy Spirit. It is not an option. We are intended to live life in the Holy Spirit's power, and only through Him is that possible. As we open ourselves and call on God to fill us with the Holy Spirit, we can be sure He will.

How do we know when the Holy Spirit is filling us? Verses 19-21 tell us. When the Holy Spirit fills us, lives in us, resides in us, He transforms our hearts. Songs of joy and praise fill our lives. We thank God for everything in Jesus' name, and we submit our wills to one another seeking the common good out of reverence for Jesus. That is the life we are called to live. That is what it means to be adolescents and adults in the life cycle of a Christian. The more we open ourselves to the Holy Spirit's filling, the more we live out of that power, the more we grow and influence those around us in Jesus' name.

For the Questions For Discussion And Growth for
Be Filled... go to page 71 now!

The Gifts (1 Corinthians 12:1-11)

The Apostle Paul offers the most extensive teaching on spiritual gifts in the New Testament. In both 1 Corinthians 12 and Romans 12 we find extended explanations of what spiritual gifts are and how they work in us to build up the body of Jesus Christ. In 1 Corinthians 12:1-11, Paul tells us how we can be sure we have the Holy Spirit in our lives and some of the gifts He gives:

[1]Now about spiritual gifts, brothers, I do not want you to be ignorant. [2]You know that when you were pagans, somehow or other you were influenced and led astray to mute idols. [3]Therefore I tell you that no one who is speaking by the Spirit of God says, "Jesus be cursed," and no one can say, "Jesus is Lord," except by the Holy Spirit.

⁴There are different kinds of gifts, but the same Spirit. ⁵There are different kinds of service, but the same Lord. ⁶There are different kinds of working, but the same God works all of them in all men.

⁷Now to each one the manifestation of the Spirit is given for the common good. ⁸To one there is given through the Spirit the message of wisdom, to another the message of knowledge by means of the same Spirit, ⁹to another faith by the same Spirit, to another gifts of healing by that one Spirit, ¹⁰to another miraculous powers, to another prophecy, to another distinguishing between spirits, to another speaking in different kinds of tongues, and to still another the interpretation of tongues. ¹¹All these are the work of one and the same Spirit, and he gives them to each one, just as he determines. (1 Corinthians 12:1-11 NIV)

The Holy Spirit witnesses to Jesus. When the Holy Spirit is present in our lives, He gives us the power to say, "Jesus is Lord," and mean it. When the Holy Spirit lives, works and speaks in us, we cannot say, "Jesus is cursed." People have asked me, "How can I be sure I have the Holy Spirit?" 1 Corinthians 12:3 is one of the surest biblical answers to that question!

In verses 4-6, Paul shows us how the Triune God displays His presence in us. The Holy Spirit gives us gifts. Jesus moves us to service. God, the Father, activates various kinds of works in our lives. Paul shows us that our lives are intended to be "poured out" or given away in serving others so God—Father, Son and Holy Spirit—may be glorified and others may come to know His life in them as well.

In verses 7-11 Paul offers us a list of various gifts the Holy Spirit gives. In the remainder of chapter twelve, Paul tells us how the various gifts interact analogously to the parts of the human body. Just as the human body has many different parts, so does the body of Jesus Christ. Paul makes it clear that no gift is superior to another. Each is

67

needed to build up the body of Jesus Christ and to extend His influence in the world. The gifts listed in verses 7-11 range from the miraculous to the seemingly mundane. Many have written books about spiritual gifts; and many spiritual gift inventories and assessments are available to help believers discern their spiritual gifts, so we will not go into detail here. What we must do is make the connection between verses 4-6 and 7-11—God gifts us to serve! No matter what gift or gifts God gives through the Spirit, the goal is not that we may be honored or set apart for acclaim because of the gifts. *We are set apart to serve one another—and the greater human family—that all may become brothers and sisters through our Lord, Jesus Christ.* As we discern and use the gifts, growth is inevitable. If we do not discern and use the Holy Spirit's gifts growth stagnates. Living life in the Holy Spirit is a matter of receiving the Spirit and then responding to His presence and power, with ongoing acts of faithfulness and obedience.

For the Questions For Discussion And Growth for
The Gifts... go to page 71 now!

Questions For Discussion And Growth

Introduction: Jesus' Presence In Daily Life

How do you respond to the statement that discipleship is impossible apart from the presence of the Holy Spirit in the disciple's life?

What is your understanding of the current work of the Holy Spirit in the Church (meaning God's people around the world) *today*? How do you support that understanding through Scripture?

What does it mean to you to have Jesus' presence in your daily life?

The Promise Of The Holy Spirit (Acts 1:3b-5)

Do the Scriptures presented make the case that the promise of God is the Holy Spirit? Why or why not?

Do you see this promise as being for all people who would ever become followers of Jesus? On what Scriptures do you base your answer?

Have you received the promised Holy Spirit? If so, what is the evidence in your life? If not, what is keeping you from receiving Him?

Wait. Receive Power. Go. (Acts 1:8)

What aspect of "Wait. Receive Power. Go." is hardest for you? Why?

Think of a time when you knew that you had received the power of the Holy Spirit. How did you go in response to that?

What kind of "flashlight" are you? What do you need to do to be able to "illuminate the darkness"?

Be Filled... (Ephesians 5:15-21)

Why do you think the Apostle Paul presented his instruction regarding being filled with the Holy Spirit in the context of acknowledging that the world around us is evil?

What is the most significant aspect of Paul's command to "be filled with the Holy Spirit" to you? Why?

What do you need to do for your life to be lived consistently in a state of "fullness" in the Holy Spirit?

The Gifts... (1 Corinthians 12:1-11)

Why do you suppose that the Apostle Paul offered this litmus test for the Holy Spirit's presence in our lives in 1 Corinthians 12:3?

How does 1 Corinthians 12:4-6 help you see God as Three-in-One (The Trinity)? How does He work in us as Three-in-One?

Do you know what your spiritual gifts are? Look at 1 Corinthians 12:7-11 and see whether you recognize any of those as your gifts? Discuss this list with a family member or your home group and see whether they discern any of the gifts in you.

6

The Vital Role Of Encouragement And Accountability

"17 As iron sharpens iron, so a friend sharpens a friend."
(Proverbs 27:17 NLT)

Introduction: Living In Jesus Is a Joint Venture

From the beginning of Jesus' ministry, He gathered followers and lived life with them. The Christian adventure is not a solo endeavor. Jesus encouraged the disciples to live in community and to carry out ministry together. When He sent them out, He always sent them by twos, never alone. As we will see through the Scriptures in this chapter, both the Old and New Testament affirm that the life of faith is a life together. One of the classic works on this truth was written by Dietrich Bonhoeffer, a German pastor and theologian, who was arrested during World War II for his participation in resisting Hitler's program of world domination. The book is titled *Life Together*. Even though it was addressed to pastors, the ideas Bonhoeffer presented offer a helpful understanding of what it means to encourage and challenge one another to grow as followers of Jesus Christ. This chapter and the next, which focuses on mentoring, remind us that if we are serious about growing in the life cycle of a Christian, we must find others who are on the same journey, and live it together!

For the Questions For Discussion And Growth for
Introduction: Living in Jesus is a Joint Venture go to page 86 now!

As Iron Sharpens Iron (Proverbs 27:17)

"¹⁷As iron sharpens iron, so a friend sharpens a friend" (Proverbs 27:17 NLT).

King Solomon tells us that friends are essential to growth. The image he used reminds us that those we call friends in Jesus may not always tell us what we want to hear. When iron sharpens iron sparks fly! When friends in Jesus "sharpen" one another—hold one another accountable—tension and friction sometimes result. This chapter's title is "The Vital Role of Encouragement and Accountability." We require both encouragement and accountability to be sharpened as Jesus' followers. Sometimes life hits us hard and we get discouraged. When we do, we need friends in Jesus who will encourage us, remind us to take the high road, and help us to remember the blessings we have known along the way. At other times, when we are heading away from Jesus, when we have forgotten His commands and have decided to take control of our own lives, we need friends in Jesus who will call us to account. Friendship that sharpens never gives up nor lets go of us, even when we have given up and are letting go of God. Do you have such a friend or friends in your life? If you do, thank God for them every day and pray God's continued growth for those relationships. If you do not, ask God to provide such a friend or friends. A couple of simple cautions: These friends need to be of the same gender. Sometimes we have difficulty distinguishing between spiritual and sexual feelings and attitudes, so it is vital not to confuse them by developing encouragers and accountability partners of the opposite gender. (Unless of course, they are our spouses!) Remember your accountability partner is not responsible **for** you. He or she is responsible **to** you. It will not be your accountability partner's fault if you fall. It will be yours. Your accountability partner can certainly forgive you for offenses you commit against him or her, but only Jesus can forgive sin. I point out these simple cautions because our accountability partners can help us grow, but they cannot take the place of God in our lives.

> For the Questions For Discussion And Growth for
> *As Iron Sharpens Iron* go to page 87 now!

The Inner Circle: Peter, James and John (Mark 9:2-4)

During my seminary years, I was told by several professors that when I became a pastor life would become extremely lonely. They said I would not be able to have close friends in the congregation I served. Their reasoning went like this: To invest in a close friendship or accountability relationship with members of the congregation would be too dangerous. If the friend ever "turned on you," he would know things that could "hurt the church" if divulged. In addition, I was told that having close friends among church members would upset other members since I needed to treat them all the same. As I reflected on this advice, I could not help thinking about Jesus. Jesus not only chose twelve disciples with whom He invested more time than with anyone else; He also had an inner circle of three men: Peter, James and John. They were able to see and do things the other nine disciples did not. One example of this is found in Mark 9:2-4:

> [2]Six days later Jesus took Peter, James, and John, and led them up a high mountain to be alone. As the men watched, Jesus' appearance was transformed, [3]and his clothes became dazzling white, far whiter than any earthly bleach could ever make them. [4]Then Elijah and Moses appeared and began talking with Jesus. (Mark 9:2-4 NLT)

This amazing event, which is referred to as The Transfiguration, was witnessed only by "the inner circle." The other nine disciples were down in the valley futilely attempting to drive a demon out of a boy. Peter, James and John sat in the front row for one of the most incredible events ever witnessed by human eyes. Why? Why did

75

Jesus select an inner circle? Why did the others have to stay below?
Is this model for us in our growth as Jesus' followers? I don't know
the answer to all of those questions, but the answer to the final
question seems obvious: "Yes." Jesus invested more time in Peter,
James and John, because they would become the leaders of the group
and because He apparently had a greater affinity for them. John refers
to himself as "the disciple Jesus loved," which is not code for Jesus
and John having an inappropriate attraction to one another. It is a
simple statement of the reality of all human relationships: We
respond to other people differently. For Jesus or a pastor or **anyone**
to attempt to treat everyone the same or love everyone the same is to
fail to account for human differences. While Jesus is especially fond
of each one of us, as He walked the earth He developed a closer
relationship with three people than with anyone else. They were
included in conversations and events only they experienced. You and
I are also going to find some people in life, maybe just one or two,
with whom we bond more closely than others. That reality will either
accelerate or stymie our growth as Jesus' followers. If our inner
circle consists of growing followers of Jesus, who challenge us to
grow as well, then our growth will be bolstered. If our inner circle
does not know Jesus or is not committed to becoming more like Him,
our growth will be held back.   While the traits of others that cause
them to be natural matches as members of our inner circle cannot be
calculated or planned, we must be intentional about the process of
developing our inner circle. In the end, that inner circle will have a
great deal of influence on who we become.

For the Questions For Discussion And Growth for
The Inner Circle: Peter, James And John go to page 87 now!

Jesus And Peter

Of the three members of Jesus' inner circle, Peter gets the most print. He seems to have been quite impetuous in serving Jesus, at least before he received the Holy Spirit on the day of Pentecost! We turn now to several examples of Peter's interactions with Jesus and how they show us the vital role of encouragement and accountability in our growth as Jesus' followers.

Jesus And Peter: You Are The Christ... (Matthew 16:15-19)

In our first encounter, Jesus had asked the disciples who the crowds thought He was. The disciples had offered various responses: Elijah, John the Baptist, Jeremiah. Then Jesus made the question more personal. He asked the disciples who they said He was. We pick up the encounter with Jesus' question and Peter's response.

> [15]Then he asked them, "But who do you say I am?"
>
> [16]Simon Peter answered, "You are the Messiah, the Son of the living God."
>
> [17]Jesus replied, "You are blessed, Simon son of John, because my Father in heaven has revealed this to you. You did not learn this from any human being. [18]Now I say to you that you are Peter (which means 'rock'), and upon this rock I will build my church, and all the powers of hell will not conquer it. [19]And I will give you the keys of the Kingdom of Heaven. Whatever you forbid on earth will be forbidden in heaven, and whatever you permit on earth will be permitted in heaven." (Matthew 16:15-19 NLT)

How did Jesus encourage Peter? Incredibly! He told Peter, "You are blessed, Simon son of John, because my Father in heaven revealed this to you. You did not learn this from any human being." Jesus affirmed Peter's discernment and told him he was blessed. He went on to give Peter a new name—Peter. We are more used to using Peter's new name than his given name: Simon. Jesus tells Peter He will build the Church upon him ("Petra" the Greek word for Peter means rock). What an incredible affirmation and responsibility! Jesus shows us that when our friends in Him demonstrate discernment, when they boldly speak His truth, we need to encourage and affirm them.

If you have read the entire discourse from Matthew 16, you know that Jesus went on to tell Peter that He was going to be crucified. Peter rebuked Jesus and told Him that it was never going to happen. At that point, Jesus held Peter accountable. He told Peter that his thinking was wrong because he was only concerned about his own needs and not the matters of God. Sometimes when we receive affirmation we are more vulnerable to pride and other devices of Satan. Peter certainly seemed to be. Jesus did not shrink back from correcting Peter, just as He had freely offered encouragement when it was appropriate.

For the Questions For Discussion And Growth for
Jesus And Peter: You Are The Christ... go to page 88 now!

Jesus And Peter: I Will Go To Prison And Death (Luke 22:31-34)

In our next encounter between Peter and Jesus, we find Jesus and the twelve at the Last Supper. Jesus tells Peter that Satan is going to tempt the entire group and that Peter will fail him. Peter's response is what we would expect, "No way! That will never happen!" Let us look and see how Jesus deals with Peter's impulsiveness in this situation:

> [31]"Simon, Simon, Satan has asked to sift each of you like wheat. [32]But I have pleaded in prayer for you, Simon, that your faith should not fail. So when you have repented and turned to me again, strengthen your brothers."
>
> [33]Peter said, "Lord, I am ready to go to prison with you, and even to die with you."

³⁴But Jesus said, "Peter, let me tell you something. Before the rooster crows tomorrow morning, you will deny three times that you even know me." (Luke 22:31-34 NLT)

Jesus had given Peter and the rest of the disciples some disheartening news: They were going to be "sifted like wheat" by Satan. Jesus made a specific comment to Peter. He told him that He had pleaded with His Heavenly Father for Peter that his faith would not fail. Then He said, "...when you have repented and turned to me again, strengthen your brothers." This is not encouragement as we normally think of it. How **dis**couraging it must have been for Peter to hear that he would need to repent after his time of testing. But, Jesus' goal was to plant a seed of hope in Peter's mind before he failed.

Peter responded with boldness. We would expect that from what we know of his personality. He told Jesus he was ready to go to prison and even death with Jesus. At this point Jesus could have reprimanded Peter, but He did not. He knew the weight of the situation all of them faced. Instead of a reprimand or rebuke, Jesus offered a statement of fact. He let Peter know that before morning when the rooster crowed, Peter would deny three times that he even knew Jesus. That prediction came true. Peter **did** deny Jesus three times during the night. According to Luke's Gospel, as Peter was denying Jesus the third time Jesus' eyes met Peter's. How terrible that moment must have been! No words were spoken, but a surer moment of accountability has never been seen. Jesus' eyes must have spoken volumes to Peter. In that moment, Peter ran out and "wept bitterly."

For Peter, life must have seemed over. As he watched Jesus die the next day, as he sat in a locked room until Sunday morning, he must have gone over and over in his mind what Jesus had said, his response, and his actions. Jesus was dead. Peter had failed. Life no longer held meaning or purpose. Peter must have thought such things. We know differently because we live on the resurrection side of the cross. Peter would learn that truth soon enough, and his life would be renewed! In every situation, Jesus encouraged and held Peter accountable. As followers of Jesus, we are called to do the same for those in our inner circles. In order to grow, we need others who will offer honest encouragement and accountability.

For the Questions For Discussion And Growth for
Jesus And Peter: I Will Go To Prison And Death go to page 89 now!

Jesus And Peter: Feed My Sheep (John 21:15-19)

Now we turn to our final encounter between Jesus and Peter. Jesus has risen from the dead. Peter and several other disciples have gone fishing. They have fished all night and caught nothing. As day breaks, they see a man standing on the shore. He asks whether they have caught any fish. They tell him no. The man tells them to throw their nets into the water on the other side of the boat. Immediately, they catch so many fish their nets start to break. John, one of the disciples with Peter, tells him that the man on shore is Jesus. Peter dives into the water and swims to shore. When the rest of the disciples arrive, Jesus makes breakfast for them. We pick up the account with a post-breakfast conversation between Jesus and Peter:

[15]After breakfast Jesus asked Simon Peter, "Simon son of John, do you love me more than these?"

"Yes, Lord," Peter replied, "you know I love you."

"Then feed my lambs," Jesus told him.

[16]Jesus repeated the question: "Simon son of John, do you love me?"

"Yes, Lord," Peter said, "you know I love you."

"Then take care of my sheep," Jesus said.

[17]A third time he asked him, "Simon son of John, do you love me?"

Peter was hurt that Jesus asked the question a third time. He said, "Lord, you know everything. You know that I love you."

Jesus said, "Then feed my sheep. [18]"I tell you the truth, when you were young, you were able to do as you liked; you dressed yourself and went wherever you wanted to go. But when you are old, you will stretch out your hands, and others will dress you and take you where you don't want to go." [19]Jesus said this to let him know by what kind of death he would glorify God. Then Jesus told him, "Follow me." (John 21:15-19 NLT)

Three times Jesus asked Peter whether he loved Him—three times! The same number of times Peter had denied Jesus. Each time Peter responded, "Yes! I love you." The third time Jesus asked the question Peter was deeply hurt. Do you think that was Jesus' goal? Did He want to hurt Peter? No. He wanted to give Peter the opportunity to unload the tremendous burden of guilt he had been carrying. Each time Peter responded to the question with a "Yes, Lord," Jesus told Peter to feed or care for His "sheep," His people. Peter's denial of Jesus in Jesus' hour of greatest need was terrible. It was terrible, but not unforgivable. It was terrible, but not enough to disqualify him from serving Jesus. It was terrible, but not enough that Jesus would stop encouraging him and holding him accountable. Jesus reinstated Peter to ministry and called him to a life of serving in Jesus' name.

Jesus did one more thing—he told Peter that one day he would die for Him. Remember how Peter had professed that he would go to prison and death **with** Jesus? Now, Jesus affirmed that one day Peter would go to prison and death **for** Him. What an amazing piece of encouragement! It was as if Jesus said, "Peter, one day you are going to be martyred for me. You are going to remain faithful. In the end, you will not be remembered as the one who denied me but as the one who served me even to death."

Perhaps the most vital form of encouragement is a second chance! At some point each of us disappoints others—**all** others. We may vow to be faithful to Jesus, our spouses, our brothers and sisters in Jesus—even to death—but even as redeemed followers of Jesus, the fallen human nature in our lives still surfaces. Throughout the life cycle of **each** Christian, the struggle continues between living life in the Holy Spirit and reverting back to our sinful natures. Thank God that Jesus always calls us back. He reinstates us. He encourages us with the knowledge that in the end as we trust in Him and live in the power of the Holy Spirit, we **will** be faithful and experience eternity with Him. Thank God for the message of Jesus and Peter woven through the Gospels! Since Jesus stuck through it all with Peter, and he eventually became one of Jesus' most faithful messengers ever, there is always hope for you and me. A person is truly blessed to have an encourager and accountability partner like Jesus, who gives us second chances and calls us up to what God has for us, even when we think we have blown it and are of no further use to Him.

For the Questions For Discussion And Growth for
Jesus And Peter: Feed My Sheep go to page 90 now!

Barnabas And Saul (Acts 11:25-26; 13:1-5; 15:36-41)

Our final example of encouragement and accountability is Barnabas and Saul. The name Barnabas means "Son of Encouragement." No one was ever more aptly named. When Saul of Tarsus became a believer, many were skeptical of the conversion—not Barnabas! As we will see in our first of three readings from the book of Acts, Barnabas searched for Saul. He knew this converted Pharisee who had been so zealous to destroy the fellowship of Jesus Christ would be a tremendous asset to the advancement of God's kingdom. More than that, Barnabas realized Saul was a man who needed a friend and he knew he could be one. Let us turn now to Barnabas' first encounter with Saul.

> [25]Then Barnabas went on to Tarsus to look for Saul. [26]When he found him, he brought him back to Antioch. Both of them stayed there with the church for a full year, teaching large crowds of people. (It was at Antioch that the believers were first called Christians.) (Act 11:25-26 NLT)

We are not given many details about how the friendship between Barnabas and Saul developed. We do have a brief example of what it means to be an encourager. Barnabas **sought after** Saul. Encouragers look for opportunities to find those who need encouragement. When Barnabas found Saul, he brought him back to Antioch so Saul could become part of the church family. Imagine the challenge it must have been for the others to trust Saul, given his reputation. Having Barnabas vouch for him would have been a huge bonus. Similarly, we may have the opportunity to be the bridge of encouragement between the family of faith and new believers or even seekers whose reputations precede them for the wrong reasons. Barnabas and Saul stayed in Antioch a full year and taught large crowds of people. Obviously, the duo was effective. Their gifts and skills complemented and strengthened each other. As they worked together, opportunities for encouragement and holding one another accountable surely arose. Barnabas gave Saul an opportunity. Many other believers would have cast him aside had he come to them. They almost certainly would not have searched for Saul the way Barnabas did!

In our second reading from Acts, we find a group of believers who gathered on a regular basis. Five are named. As they worshiped the Lord and fasted one day the Holy Spirit spoke to them clearly and pointedly:

> [1]Among the prophets and teachers of the church at Antioch of Syria were Barnabas, Simeon (called "the black man"),

Lucius (from Cyrene), Manaen (the childhood companion of King Herod Antipas), and Saul. [2]One day as these men were worshiping the Lord and fasting, the Holy Spirit said, "Dedicate Barnabas and Saul for the special work to which I have called them." [3]So after more fasting and prayer, the men laid their hands on them and sent them on their way. [4]So Barnabas and Saul were sent out by the Holy Spirit. They went down to the seaport of Seleucia and then sailed for the island of Cyprus. [5]There, in the town of Salamis, they went to the Jewish synagogues and preached the word of God. John Mark went with them as their assistant. (Acts 13:1-5 NLT)

The Holy Spirit selected two of the five—Barnabas and Saul. An interesting point to note: For the first year or so of their association, when the two are mentioned Barnabas' name appears first. However, later in Acts 13, Saul starts to be referred to as Paul and, from that point forward, receives first billing when they are named. Barnabas did not mind because Barnabas was not about status and position. He was about building the Kingdom of God! From the moment he found Saul, he knew one day Saul would be the one to draw the crowds. That was fine with Barnabas, because his gift was encouragement, and by it he contributed greatly to building God's Kingdom. As an apparent footnote to the text, we find that John Mark went with Barnabas and Saul as their assistant. John Mark would abandon the two during that missionary journey, which sets the stage for the final encounter between Paul and Barnabas.

[36]After some time Paul said to Barnabas, "Let's go back and visit each city where we previously preached the word of the Lord, to see how the new believers are doing." [37]Barnabas agreed and wanted to take along John Mark. [38]But Paul disagreed strongly, since John Mark had deserted them in Pamphylia and had not continued with them in their work. [39]Their disagreement was so sharp that they separated. Barnabas took John Mark with him and sailed for

Cyprus. [40]Paul chose Silas, and as he left, the believers entrusted him to the Lord's gracious care. [41]Then he traveled throughout Syria and Cilicia, strengthening the churches there. (Acts 15:36-41 NLT)

It seems that Paul and Barnabas discussed their plans and decided on their actions together. On this occaosn, Paul suggested they go back and visit each city where they had preached the word of the Lord and established churches. He wanted to see how these fledgling families of God were faring on their own. The idea sounded good to Barnabas. Always the encourager, Barnabas suggested taking John Mark along on the journey. He did not say it but the implication is clear: "Let's give the lad another chance!" Paul expressed adamant opposition. He was not about to give John Mark a second chance. Doesn't that seem a bit strange, coming from a man who was given the ultimate second chance by Jesus? Barnabas would not back down from the suggestion. Paul would not back down from refusing to take John Mark along. Eventually the disagreement became so sharp that the two **separated**. Think about that. Paul had received continuous encouragement and accountability from Barnabas for several years. They had ministered side by side in both miraculous and desperate situations. They had seen thousands of people respond to the Good News of Jesus' salvation. They had been an incredible team. Even so, Barnabas purposed to give John Mark a second chance, and he did. It meant breaking partnership, but not fellowship, with Paul. Paul took Silas, and Barnabas took John Mark. Each headed out with his new partner. The result? The churches were strengthened through Syria and Cilicia—and John Mark eventually wrote a Gospel! Thank God Barnabas' gift of encouragement extended beyond Paul. Thank God that Barnabas and Paul saw the bigger picture and continued to spread the Gospel and to strengthen the churches even when they could no longer work together. Paul and Barnabas offer us many lessons in this brief encounter. How much stronger the church can be in our day as we learn that even though we may not always agree on every detail of ministry, we can still work together to build God's Kingdom. How blessed a person is to know an encourager such as Barnabas!

For the Questions For Discussion And Growth for
Barnabas And Saul go to page 91 now!

Questions For Discussion And Growth

Introduction: Living In Jesus Is A Joint Venture

Do you have someone with whom you are intentionally living life together as followers of Jesus Christ? If not, how do you think you would benefit if you did? If you do, what have been the benefits to you?

Why do you suppose that when Jesus sent the disciples out in mission He **always** sent them out by twos? What does this tell us about our work as His followers?

As Iron Sharpens Iron (Proverbs 27:17)

When you think of iron sharpening iron as an analogy for friends in Christ, what comes to mind?

Think of a time when you needed encouragement and one when you needed accountability. Was someone there to provide them? If not, how did you handle the situation? If so, how did you respond to what was offered?

List the most important traits of an encourager/accountability partner:

The Inner Circle: Peter, James And John (Mark 9:2-4)

Do you think it is good advice for a pastor, or others who have to use discretion in their work, not to have an inner circle? Why or why not?

Why do you think Jesus had an inner circle during His earthly ministry?

Do you have an inner circle? If so, what roles does it serve?

Jesus And Peter: You Are The Christ... (Matthew 16:15-19)

Are you usually more in need of encouragement or accountability? Why?

Have you ever been given a nickname or a symbolic name by an accountability partner to show his or her faith in you or hope for your future? If so, what was the name and how did it make you feel? If not, what do you think it would have done for Peter to have Jesus give him a new name?

Why do you think Jesus chose Simon Peter out of the twelve disciples to become the "Rock"?

Jesus And Peter: I Will Go To Prison And Death (Luke 22:31-34)

If you were going to make a major mistake in serving Jesus tomorrow, would you want Him to tell you about it tonight? Why or why not?

Why do you think Jesus told Peter ahead of time that he was going to deny Jesus? How could this be an act of encouragement?

How is Peter's response to Jesus like or unlike your response would have been if you were in Peter's place?

Jesus And Peter: Feed My Sheep (John 21:15-19)

Why do you think Jesus took Peter aside and personally reinstated him before returning to heaven?

Why do you think Peter was hurt that Jesus asked him three times whether he loved Him?

What do you learn about encouragement and accountability from this interaction between Jesus with Peter?

Barnabas And Saul (Acts 11:25-26; 13:1-5; 15:36-41)

Why do you think Barnabas was willing to invest in Saul's life even though others were afraid of him? When have you invested in someone who others did not think was worth the investment?

Have you ever been in a friendship that started with you being the focus, but transitioned so the other person received more attention? If so, how did you respond?

Have you ever disagreed with a brother or sister in Jesus to the point that you had to go separate ways, but were able to continue to build the kingdom of God as a result?

7

A Step Further: Mentoring

¹This letter is from Paul, an apostle of Christ Jesus, appointed by
the command of God our Savior and Christ Jesus, who gives us
hope. ²I am writing to Timothy, my true son in the faith.
(1 Timothy 1:1-2 NLT)

Introduction: Leaving A Legacy

While all of chapter 10 is devoted to leaving a legacy or seeing the
life cycle of a Christian start again in another generation, I start this
chapter on mentoring with the concept of legacy as well. Why?
Because mentoring is one of the best ways to leave a legacy!
Mentoring is nothing more or less than an intentional relationship
developed by one who is farther along the journey of growth and
maturity in the life cycle of a Christian with another who is either just
starting the journey or who is far enough behind that the mentor has
real potential for assisting the mentoree's growth. I have known the
joy of being mentored since my teenage years and have mentored
others since I was in my twenties.

My first mentor was Pastor Andy Wiegand, who came to Gipsy
Christian Church when I was in my mid-teens. At the time, I was
going through a challenging stage in my development as a follower of
Jesus. I was not attending worship. A certain, specific situation had
led to my considering most of the people in that little church in Gipsy
to be hypocrites. Of course, the assessment held some truth, since all

of us are hypocritical to one degree or another. No one except Jesus has lived the life of faith with perfection, but as a fifteen year-old, I saw everything in black and white. So, I told my mother I loved Jesus, would read my Bible every day and would still tell people about Jesus. I was just not going to attend worship anymore. By some amazing power of discernment, she agreed with me. I expected a fight, a "mandatory sentence" of continuing in worship with the hypocrites. To my surprise and relief she said, "Okay." Not long after my worship boycott began, Andy Wiegand came to serve as our pastor. I did not know it then, but my mother encouraged Andy to become friends with me. He did. Since Andy was single, Mom invited him over to our home for dinner regularly. I liked Andy. He had graduated with honors from Harvard University, where he had been a stand out tennis and squash player. Then he had come to Gipsy Christian Church in Gipsy, Pennsylvania to serve about fifty people as their pastor. That intrigued me. Let me put that a different way: I thought he was crazy, and told him so. I asked him why he had come. He told me God had called him. I asked, "What? On the phone?" He explained that it was **not** on the phone but that God had spoken to Him and called him to serve us as our lay pastor. Eventually, Andy became my mentor. We got together regularly to study the Bible, and Andy brought the book to life. He showed me how to see the life of Jesus that was already in the Gospels. He occasionally took me with him to visit folks in the hospital and to a college bible study he led. We went to a local university and played racquetball. I had never played before meeting Andy; but before long, I had become decent, and he was amazing, so we always won. I liked that.

One day after about six months of bible study, dinners and conversations, Andy asked me a simple question, "Chris, why don't you go to church?" Through his investment in my life, he had earned the right to ask the question.

I answered, "They're all hypocrites and I don't need them." Andy proceeded through a line of questioning that probed whether any hypocrites played on my high school football team or ate lunch with me in the school cafeteria. I acknowledged they did. Then Andy asked an important question,

"Do you ever act like a hypocrite?" I had to admit I did.

Finally, I asked, "Andy, what's your point?

He said, "Well, I always figured I'd rather go to church with a hypocrite than to hell with him." I went to worship the next Sunday, and have gone on most Sundays since!

I share the story of my first mentor because it shows that mentors invest in others for the others' benefit. Andy did not have to study the Bible with me or invite me to play racquetball or take me with him on hospital calls or challenge my lack of worship participation, but he did because he was investing in me and, ultimately, in the Kingdom of God. That is what mentors do. Over the years, I have had a number of excellent mentors. Now that I am in my fifties my mentors are often people I have not even met. I learn from their books, webinars, and websites. While I prefer the one-on-one exchange of in person mentoring, I have come to realize that when one is not available I can still grow deeper in maturity by the mentoring provided in resources. I wrote this book, in part, to become a mentor to others I may never meet. My prayer is that everyone who reads *Life Cycle of a Christian* will take this to heart and invest in their own spiritual growth by finding a mentor or mentors. Then, as they mature, I pray they will become mentors to others. That is leaving a legacy.

For the Questions For Discussion And Growth for *Introduction: Leaving A Legacy* go to page 101 now!

The Inner Circle Revisited   (Mark 9:2-13)

In our last chapter, I introduced Jesus' inner circle: Peter, James and John. They often received opportunities to experience Jesus' life and teaching at a deeper level than the rest of the disciples. That is what mentoring is. Mentors show their mentorees their lives up close and personal. Although the crowds heard Jesus' teaching and were amazed by it; although they received His miracles and were physically changed by them, they did not get to see Jesus transfigured with Elijah and Moses. They did not get to see Jesus raise Jairus' daughter from the dead. Only Peter, James and John experienced that. As a pastor, I am well aware of the difference between teaching, preaching and mentoring. All three are personal. All three provide the one on the receiving end with information. Only mentoring takes the mentoree into the mentor's world for the mentoree's personal growth and development. Jesus was able to mentor three men at a time. We may also be able to do that, but the more typical mentoring situation is one-on-one. Let us look again at the Transfiguration of Jesus and see how he used it to invest in Peter, James and John's lives and futures. This passage includes Jesus' interaction with the inner circle after the transfiguration ended.

[2]Six days later Jesus took Peter, James, and John, and led them up a high mountain to be alone. As the men watched, Jesus' appearance was transformed, [3]and his clothes became dazzling white, far whiter than any earthly bleach could ever make them. [4]Then Elijah and Moses appeared and began talking with Jesus.

[5]Peter exclaimed, "Rabbi, it's wonderful for us to be here! Let's make three shelters as memorials—one for you, one for Moses, and one for Elijah." [6]He said this because he didn't really know what else to say, for they were all terrified.

95

⁷Then a cloud overshadowed them, and a voice from the cloud said, "This is my dearly loved Son. Listen to him." ⁸Suddenly, when they looked around, Moses and Elijah were gone, and only Jesus was with them.

⁹As they went back down the mountain, he told them not to tell anyone what they had seen until the Son of Man had risen from the dead. ¹⁰So they kept it to themselves, but they often asked each other what he meant by "rising from the dead."

¹¹Then they asked him, "Why do the teachers of religious law insist that Elijah must return before the Messiah comes?"

¹²Jesus responded, "Elijah is indeed coming first to get everything ready for the Messiah. Yet, why do the Scriptures say that the Son of Man must suffer greatly and be treated with utter contempt? ¹³But I tell you, Elijah has already come, and they chose to abuse him, just as the Scriptures predicted." (Mark 9:2-13 NLT)

Consider the interaction between Jesus and the three. Peter was overcome by the event. He wanted to pitch tents and stay on the mountaintop forever to enjoy the incredible experience. God told the three that Jesus was His Son, the one He loved, and that they should listen to Him. Then it was over. They started down the mountain, back to "reality." As they walked, Jesus told the three to keep the event secret until He rose from the dead. They agreed but did not have a clue what Jesus meant by rising from the dead. Then the questions started to fly. The first one was, "Why do the religious teachers say Elijah has to come before the Messiah does?" They had just seen Elijah. They believed that Jesus was the Messiah. The events were not in the right order. Jesus cleared it up for them. Elijah had come, and the people had abused him. Jesus was referring to John the Baptizer. This shows us that mentors provide opportunities for their mentorees' growth not afforded to others. In fact, Jesus specifically forbade the three from telling anyone about the event until He had risen from the dead. Mentors and mentorees share insights and experiences that lead the mentorees to grow deeper and richer in their understanding of Jesus. Sometimes those experiences are not fully understood until later.

I remember asking Andy Wiegand how a person knows when he has been called to serve as a pastor. Andy said, "When God calls someone to be a pastor, He gives him a vision of the church." I was seventeen. I did not know what Andy meant at that moment. Ten years later I did. Five years after that I understood even more; and, today, I would say the very same thing to anyone who asked me that question. God does give people a vision for the church when He calls them as leaders in the church. Mentoring accelerates the mentorees' growth and development. That is why each of us needs a mentor.

For the Questions For Discussion And Growth for
The Inner Circle Revisited go to page 102 now!

Barnabas And Saul Revisited

Let us turn to Barnabas and Saul once again. Barnabas was definitely Saul's mentor at the outset of their relationship. While Saul was a Pharisee and undoubtedly possessed one of the most brilliant minds of their day, Barnabas was already a believer in Jesus. He was living the life and was committed to developing other leaders. Barnabas was an intentional mentor, and he could demonstrate living the life in Jesus. We know he mentored Paul and John Mark. We may reasonably assume he mentored many others during his lifetime as well.

While the Bible does not tell us why Barnabas sought out Saul, he must have seen Saul as a potential boon for the kingdom of God with his rabbinical training, zealous nature, and passion for doing God's will. Saul had shown those traits even when he was wrong about what God's will was and persecuted the church. All these things contributed to Barnabas' recognition of Saul as a potential candidate for mentoring. If you add the practical matter of other believers fearing Saul, Barnabas was most likely the only one lining up to mentor Saul. As you consider finding a mentor—or being a mentor— pray. Ask God to show you who in your life or sphere of influence could be the right person to serve you or under whom you may serve as a mentor. Do not settle on the obvious candidate immediately. After all, Saul certainly was not the obvious candidate for Barnabas. We could say that John Mark, a mission team drop-out, was not an obvious choice either! While most of the examples we have in the Bible show a mentor seeking a mentoree, remember that wise followers of Jesus search for mentors because they know a mentor will help them accelerate their growth.

My second important mentor, Arthur Pace, served as a supervising pastor when I was a first year seminarian at Princeton Theological Seminary. Arthur and I hit it off immediately when I interviewed at the church he served in Garwood, New Jersey. One of the most valuable insights Arthur passed on to me was so simple, yet it has increased my ability to learn by 100% over the years. As we started our year of working together, Arthur said, "Chris, over the next year I'm going to do a lot of things right. If you watch and learn from them, you will be a more effective pastor in years to come." Then he said, "I will also do a lot of things wrong. If you dismiss me because I'm not perfect, then you will miss the opportunity to learn from those things as well. If you learn from them, then you won't have to make the same mistakes yourself! That way, no matter what I do, you can learn from me." You may have already discovered that truth. As a twenty-three year old seminarian, learning from others' mistakes was a new concept for me. Over the years, it has served me well since everyone makes mistakes and it is much wiser to learn from them than to repeat them yourself!

For the Questions For Discussion And Growth for *Barnabas And Saul Revisited* go to page 102 now!

Paul And Timothy (2 Timothy 2:1-2)

One of the most documented mentoring relationships in the New Testament is that of the Apostle Paul with Timothy. Paul referred to Timothy as his "dear son," not only in the letters addressed to Timothy but in others as well. One of the most valuable teachings Paul presented to Timothy in the area of mentoring is found in 2 Timothy 2:1-2:

> [1]Timothy, my dear son, be strong through the grace that God gives you in Christ Jesus. [2]You have heard me teach things that have been confirmed by many reliable witnesses. Now teach these truths to other trustworthy people who will be able to pass them on to others. (2 Timothy 2:1-2 NLT)

First, Paul mentored Timothy. Now Timothy was to mentor others who would mentor others. This is how the legacy of faith is passed from one generation to the next. It also reminds us that we may be in a "mentoring up" or a "mentoring down" relationship at any given time. Paul was still instructing Timothy. Thus, Timothy was in a "mentoring up" situation with Paul, that is, Timothy was the mentoree. At the same time, he was being called to mentor others, a "mentoring down" situation. Here Paul tells Timothy that he is to be in both situations at once. One of the basic principles in the Bible is that *we are blessed to be a blessing* (See Genesis 12:1-3). When we have received a mentor's training, heart and blessing, the only responsible response as followers of Jesus is to pass them on to someone else. Imagine what would happen in our lives if **all** of us did this! The truth is if **all** of us did it, and we only mentored one new

99

person a year, who mentored one new person a year, in 32 years there would be 8,589,934,592 (more than 8.5 **billion**) followers of Jesus on the planet. Wow! No wonder Jesus and Paul thought mentoring was so vital!

For the Questions For Discussion And Growth for
Paul And Timothy go to page 103 now!

Internal Mentoring

In introducing this chapter, I mentioned I have received mentoring from books, webinars and other resources. Another source of mentoring in our lives is *Internal Mentoring*. By that I mean the Holy Spirit will lead and guide us, will mentor us, as we study God's word, reflect on the teachings and writings of others, and as we live out our faith in practical ways every day. While mentors are vital to our growth and development as followers of Jesus, in the end each of us is responsible for our own growth and development. As I have taught our children since they were quite young, the purpose of all formal learning is to develop the attitude and habit of self-learning. While many of us may think that it is the pastor's job or the teacher's job or the mentor's job to see that we grow and develop, that responsibility belongs to only one person after we move along the life cycle of a Christian from childhood into adolescence and adulthood—you (and me). While we need pastors, teachers and mentors, while we need one another to encourage us and hold us accountable, while we need to worship together on a regular basis, in the end the Holy Spirit is our pastor, teacher, mentor and accountability partner. No matter how many folks we have in our entourage of growth partners, we all have times when we are alone. Who leads us then? Who holds us accountable then? When you are alone in a motel room while on a business trip, or with a group of non-believers at a school function or driving down the road and someone cuts you off—who holds you accountable? The Holy Spirit. He is our ever-present mentor. Remember that. We never outgrow our need for mentors, but as we mature in our walk with Jesus, we do come to the place where the Holy Spirit becomes more and more the one we turn to for that mentoring. He is the only mentor who never leads us astray nor lets us down and is **always** with us!

For the Questions For Discussion And Growth for *Internal Mentoring* go to page 104 now!

Questions For Discussion And Growth

Introduction: Leaving A Legacy

Have you ever had a mentor? If so, what have you gained from that experience?

List the ways that Andy Wiegand served as a mentor to me during my teenage years. (This list will serve to aid you in being a mentor or providing a ministry description for a mentor for you.)

Have you ever thought of books, DVD's and such as mentors? Do you agree that they can serve in that way? Why or why not?

The Inner Circle Revisited (Mark 9:2-13)

What do you learn about mentoring from Jesus' interaction with the disciples in Mark 9:2-13?

Why do mentors sometimes give us answers that we do not understand at the moment? How can this help us grow as followers of Jesus?

Barnabas And Saul Revisited

Why do you think Barnabas chose Saul to mentor? Why would he choose John Mark? What do we learn from these choices?

If you are not in a mentoring relationship right now and are far enough along the life cycle of a Christian to be a mentor but are not, who would you think of immediately as a potential mentor and a potential mentoree?

Paul And Timothy (2 Timothy 2:1-2)

Are you currently in "mentoring up" and "mentoring down" relationships?   If so, how are you encouraging the person(s) you are mentoring to continue the mentoring legacy?

Why do you think relatively few people take the Apostle Paul's charge to Timothy to "mentor down" seriously?

Does acknowledging the 8.5 billion people who could be mentored in the next 32 years help you see the potential of mentoring? What are you going to do about it?

Internal Mentoring

How are you taking steps to make the Holy Spirit your primary mentor?

How will it impact your life when the Holy Spirit is your primary mentor?

8

Why Some Christians Never Grow

*6*We know that our old sinful selves were crucified with Christ so that sin might lose its power in our lives. We are no longer slaves to sin. (Romans 6:6 NLT)

Introduction: Stumbling Blocks Along the Way

If you have made it this far, you must be serious about growing into maturity as a Jesus follower. Many folks never grow up in the faith. They remain infants or children all their lives. Why? Many reasons could be given, but Rick Warren has a saying that has influenced me deeply over the years and, which may be the best explanation: **We become what we are committed to in life.** Those who grow up to be spiritual giants—the John Wesleys, the Charles Spurgeons, the Billy Grahams—did so by committing their lives fully to Jesus. They invested their lives in learning God's word, in prayer and in developing systems and people who would keep their visions going after they had or have gone on to receive their rewards in heaven. What about those who intended to be great followers of Jesus, who intended to influence hundreds, thousands or millions for Jesus—but never did or never have? What happened to them? Instead of committing to their intentions, they committed to excuses, stumbling blocks, or detours along the way.

I have been guilty of letting obstacles and excuses keep me from growing at times. I was born and raised in Gipsy, Pennsylvania. If you have never heard of it, you are among a vast majority of people in the world! My dad and many of my friends' dads were coal miners and laborers. Few earned college educations. Most of them worked hard all their lives and instilled honesty and hard work as virtues in their children. In general, they did not see themselves as great men of God. My dad was an angry man who did not know God at all until just a few years before his death. I point out all that so you may see that my early vision of life was not to change the world in Jesus' name. My early vision was not to share the new life of Jesus Christ with the world—one person at a time. All I really wanted to do was get out of Gipsy, go to college, get a job that would make me rich and famous—or at least rich—and marry someone who would make me happy. The goal of pursuing riches and fame stood as an obstacle in my life for a long time. Thinking that my wife was supposed to make me happy stood as a stumbling block for a long time, too. That I did not develop the ability to think in terms of plans and systems, because God blessed me with native intelligence and I had inherited my dad's strong work ethic and anger, has also stood as a stumbling block in the long run. Not that plans and systems have ever saved anyone, but they certainly have helped people reach more people and present the Good News of Jesus to them more effectively!

Although I have grown a great deal as a follower of Jesus since receiving Him as my Savior and Lord at age twelve and have relied on the Holy Spirit to empower me to serve faithfully as a pastor and preacher for nearly twenty-five years, until recently I have not come close to fully impacting others for God's Kingdom in the ways God has gifted me to do. Why? Instead of pursuing God's plan for my life with all the intentionality and zeal I possessed, I have allowed excuses and stumbling blocks to hold me back—and I am **deeply** committed to growing as a follower of Jesus.

What about those who have been born again but saw being born again as nothing more or less than a means to gaining heaven someday rather than the start of a life-long pursuit of God and growing up into the full stature of Jesus Christ? For them, growing is not a matter of importance or urgency. Their conscious thoughts do not dwell on such things on a daily basis. Other pursuits stand in the way of growing up as followers of Jesus, and those pursuits win the allegiance of their commitments. I do not say this to be judgmental at all. On the contrary, I understand it fully. I say it in the hope of arring those in such pursuits back to the **one** pursuit—Jesus.

We will look at only two Scriptures in this chapter. The first comes from Jesus' mouth. It is the familiar Parable of the Sower (Soils). In t, Jesus presents the stumbling blocks to growth we **all** face. The econd Scripture comes from the Apostle Paul's letter to the Romans. n it, we will see that whether we grow or continue in sin is a matter of choice and commitment. I pray that as we read these Scriptures and reflect on them we will see the obstacles and excuses in our own ives for what they are, and by God's Spirit within us commit to vercoming them!

For the Questions For Discussion And Growth for
Introduction: Stumbling Blocks Along The Way go to page 116 now!

The Parable Of The Sower (Mark 4:1-9)

Sometimes when we read familiar teachings of Jesus, the full mpact of the teaching is lost. We may have heard the teaching many imes since we were children and we "know" the point. We skim hrough such teachings on our way to other passages that are not as amiliar, or that hold greater personal interest. As we turn to the Parable of the Sower, pause and reflect on the potential stumbling locks it presents. Instead of reading straight through, we will take one point at a time and then reflect on the truth Jesus offers.

¹Once again Jesus began teaching by the lakeshore. A very large crowd soon gathered around him, so he got into a boat. Then he sat in the boat while all the people remained on the shore. ²He taught them by telling many stories in the form of parables, such as this one: (Mark 4:1-2 NLT)

In these introductory comments, we see that Jesus drew a large crowd, as he usually did. Think about that for a moment. Jesus **always** drew crowds, yet in the end only a relatively few responded to His call to a new life. Why? The new life requires tremendous, supernatural transformation. Such a concept seems inconceivable. How could God transform us? After all, we were born in _[wherever we were born]_ … did not have the right teachers … did not have wealthy parents ... _[whatever our excuse]_ . The crowds loved to hear Jesus' stories. They loved to receive the food He provided so miraculously. They loved to be healed and to have their demons exorcised, but they did not love the consequences of following Him, of moving from fascination to commitment. Being born again is a gift. God gives it to all who come to Him. *Growing in Jesus is another matter altogether. It requires great commitment—the kind of commitment most of us only invest in grades, sports or climbing the corporate ladder.* We bring God our leftovers and wonder why we fail to grow. The church has often contributed to our lack of growth by expecting so little of us. Jesus told the crowds the truth: Following me will cost you everything, and following me will give you everything!

³"Listen! A farmer went out to plant some seed. ⁴As he scattered it across his field, some of the seed fell on a footpath, and the birds came and ate it. (Mark 4:3-4 NLT)

If you know the parable, you know the seed that fell on the footpath represents those who hear the word of God, but never even begin to grow. The devil snatches them away first. Satan. He factors in as a major obstacle to growth in Jesus from the very beginning to the very end of the life cycle of a Christian. I have not spoken much about

108

him, because I know when we commit our hearts, minds, souls and strength to loving God and one another Satan holds no power in our lives. The goal of this book is to emphasize how we grow. Therefore, I have accentuated the positive. We must acknowledge Satan, though, because he does exist. He does have power. The world runs after his deceitful counterfeits of God's blessings. Sin—his domain—is fun. Otherwise, no one would sin. The stumbling blocks he lays before us entice us to give the best of ourselves to the worst. We will study more about that when we move to Romans 6. Suffice it to say, if Satan plucks away the seed before it can grow in our lives, we will not grow.

> [5]Other seed fell on shallow soil with underlying rock. The seed sprouted quickly because the soil was shallow. [6]But the plant soon wilted under the hot sun, and since it didn't have deep roots, it died. (Mark 4:5-6 NLT)

Here we have the Christian who rejoices in being born again and grows quickly through infancy, maybe even making it to childhood. But he does not sink roots of faith deep enough into the soil to drink deeply of the Spirit. When the hot sun shines, the faith withers and dies. I experienced this once, literally, when I was a child. I decided to plant radishes because I knew my dad loved them. I made a bad decision, though, about where to plant them. Instead of clearing some ground and planting them there, I took some sand from my sandbox, and put it in a wooden trailer that sat in our back yard. The sand was only about two inches deep, so the radishes sprouted quickly. I watered them when I remembered, but one day I came out and every single radish was dead. The little leaves had withered and shriveled up to virtually nothing. I could not understand why. Years later, Jesus' parable cleared it up for me. A wooden trailer is the same as rocky soil, so the plants could not establish roots. Jesus tells us the rocky soil and the hot sun are the problems and persecution that all believers encounter. When we experience problems and persecution, we often think they will stunt our growth. The opposite is true—if our roots are going down deep. They will kill us spiritually if we do not have deep roots. If we do, they only make us stronger. The next time troubles come, the next time someone hassles you because you serve Jesus, thank God for the opportunity to grow and to sink your roots down deeper in Jesus!

> [7]Other seed fell among thorns that grew up and choked out the tender plants so they produced no grain. (Mark 4:7 NLT)

The thorny soil may be the most typical soil type for Jesus' followers who live in America. Jesus tells us the thorns are the worries about this life, the lure of wealth and other things. How many times has a Jesus follower been derailed from growth by such things? Some Christians never grow because they have committed themselves to lives of worry, pursuing wealth or other things. Other things might include addictions, distractions and dysfunctional relationships. If we want to grow up into the full stature of Jesus Christ, then we must be intentional about keeping our soil free of thorns.

> [8]Still other seeds fell on fertile soil, and they sprouted, grew, and produced a crop that was thirty, sixty, and even a hundred times as much as had been planted!" [9]Then he said, "Anyone with ears to hear should listen and understand." (Mark 4:8-9 NLT)

The parable ends with good news! Some seed falls on fertile soil and reproduces exponentially. That is the kind of life we want as Jesus' followers. To take Jesus' agricultural image a little farther, anyone who has ever raised a garden knows that even fertile soil takes work to maintain. The growing process depletes the soil, so it must be renewed. Weeds tend to infest fertile ground and must be pulled or killed by other means. Being healthy and growing as a follower of Jesus never happens by accident. As we have said from the outset, it is always intentional. Indeed, we do become what we are committed to in life, so let us commit ourselves to growing and reproducing that growth in others!

For the Questions For Discussion And Growth for
The Parable Of The Sower go to page 117 now!

Slaves To Sin Or Righteousness (Romans 6:1-16)

The heading for this section tells us that whether a person grows as a follower of Jesus is determined by whether the person commits to being a "slave to sin" or a "slave to righteousness." The Apostle Paul's reasoning sometimes seems rather academic, but here he uses a series of analogies to show us that committing to a life of sin as a follower of Jesus makes absolutely no sense. While we may say, "No kidding!" when we first read that statement, far too many of us are caught up in slavery to various sins and never become the fully mature followers Jesus calls us to be. Some Christians do not grow because they feed the life of sin instead of the life in Jesus. The struggle we experience to overcome sin and let righteousness rule in our lives never ends. As we commit to putting Jesus first, and living in the Spirit's power, victory in the struggle becomes more and more frequent. Let us look now at Paul's instruction regarding growing in the ways of righteousness from Romans 6:

> [1]Well then, should we keep on sinning so that God can show us more and more of his wonderful grace? [2]Of course not! Since we have died to sin, how can we continue to live in it? [3]Or have you forgotten that when we were joined with Christ Jesus in baptism, we joined him in his death? [4]For we died and were buried with Christ by baptism. And just as Christ was raised from the dead by the glorious power of the Father, now we also may live new lives. (Romans 6:1-4 NLT)

Paul asks an interesting question, "Since we love to sin and God loves to forgive sin, shouldn't we just go on sinning?" His answer is

"Of course not!" In the Greek language, the response is the strongest possible negative. One of my seminary professors said the only way to get the full power of the response is to translate it, "Hell, **no**!" Paul's logic is impeccable: If we have **died** to sin, how can we continue to live in it? That makes perfect sense! When we are dead to anything, it seems reasonable to assume that it is gone from our lives.

Next, Paul points out that when we are baptized we are joined with Jesus in His death. The immersion of our bodies in water symbolizes our death to sin. Finally, he tells us that just as Christ was raised from the dead by the glorious power of the Father, we may live **new** lives. Paul's image reminds us of being born again and of living in victory over sin. Such an image is a powerful call to life and growth as Jesus' followers. The question becomes whether we live the new life we have received in Jesus or remain stuck in the old one. If we answer that question with life in Jesus, we grow. If we answer it with remaining stuck in the old life, we stagnate or worse.

> [5]Since we have been united with him in his death, we will also be raised to life as he was. [6]We know that our old sinful selves were crucified with Christ so that sin might lose its power in our lives. We are no longer slaves to sin. [7]For when we died with Christ we were set free from the power of sin. [8]And since we died with Christ, we know we will also live with him. [9]We are sure of this because Christ was raised from the dead, and he will never die again. Death no longer has any power over him. [10]When he died, he died once to break the power of sin. But now that he lives, he lives for the glory of God. [11]So you also should consider yourselves to be dead to the power of sin and alive to God through Christ Jesus. (Romans 6:5-11 NLT)

Paul takes the baptism analogy and extends it. He tells us our old sinful selves were crucified with Christ so sin might lose its power over us. While Jesus emphasized being born again, Paul focused on dying to the old self. Both are necessary in order to grow up as followers of Jesus. Paul offers Jesus' actual resurrection and assurance of His never dying again as the power source for death to the power of sin and life to God through Christ Jesus. The last phrase is crucial: **through Christ Jesus.** We cannot overcome death or sin on our own. Jesus alone does that. Now, **through** Jesus Christ's presence in our lives we may live lives of victory over sin. Do we believe that? Some do and some do not. Some believe it, and act as if it is true in their lives; but there is no accompanying transformation to holiness. Those outside the church rightly see that as hypocrisy. At the other extreme are those who say even though Jesus died for our sins, the power of sin is so great we will never overcome it until we die and go to heaven. The grain of truth in this statement is that **we** will never overcome sin! Only **through** Jesus Christ living in does that happen.

> [12]Do not let sin control the way you live; do not give in to sinful desires. [13]Do not let any part of your body become an instrument of evil to serve sin. Instead, give yourselves completely to God, for you were dead, but now you have new life. So use your whole body as an instrument to do what is right for the glory of God. (Romans 6:12-13 NLT)

Paul reminds us that Jesus living in us is the only hope of overcoming sin. He also points out that we have a significant part to play: We must not give in to sinful desires nor let any part of our bodies become instruments of evil to serve sin. In his book *The Normal Christian Life*, Watchman Nee offers a great illustration of the second part of Paul's challenge to us. Since Paul tells us not to let any part of our bodies become instruments of evil to serve sin, Nee tells us when the sin involves using our hands, we should respond, "I don't have any hands." As we refuse to let our hands, feet, eyes, ears or **any** part of our bodies be used as instruments of sin, we overcome sin in our lives. You may be thinking, "It is not that easy." Neither Paul nor Nee said anything about it being easy. They simply said we

113

must not give in to sin. James reminds us that when we resist the devil he will flee from us. (See James 4:7) God will always do His part: He provided Jesus' death in our place as the source of salvation and continues to provide the Holy Spirit to empower us to live in His ways. We must do our part: Resist the devil and do not give in to sin. My experience has always been that the easiest way to resist the devil and overcome sin is to immerse myself in God! It is very difficult to pray and sin at the same time or to show the love of Jesus to others while sinning against them.

"[14]Sin is no longer your master, for you no longer live under the requirements of the law. Instead, you live under the freedom of God's grace" (Romans 6:14 NLT).

Paul makes an astute observation. Before our rebirth, sin was our master. Sin ruled and reigned in our lives. We could work hard to become better people, and it may appear to have worked, but deep in our hearts, the ruler was still sin. Now we have been set free from sin and the requirements of the law. Freedom from the requirements of the law means we do not have to live up to all the rules and regulations found there, because we live under the freedom of God's grace. That does not mean we can continue in sin! Neither our sin nor **our** goodness earns punishment or blessing from God. His goodness in Jesus has bought our salvation, and now we may live freely in it. If we rely on **our** goodness, God's only option is to find us guilty, because our goodness is never good enough. The penalty for that guilty verdict in our lives is separation from God in hell forever. That is why rebirth is crucial, and why depending on God for our growth is the only way to assure we will grow.

[15]Well then, since God's grace has set us free from the law, does that mean we can go on sinning? Of course not! [16]Don't you realize that you become the slave of whatever you choose to obey? You can be a slave to sin, which leads to

death, or you can choose to obey God, which leads to righteous living. (Romans 6:15-16 NLT)

Paul concludes by reminding us once again that we cannot go on sinning because we live under grace. Then he asks a pointed question: *Don't you realize you become the slave of whatever you choose to obey?* As God's free people, we may only become enslaved voluntarily. God has set us free from sin and death in Jesus Christ. Now we have the freedom to choose our master: God or sin. It sounds so simple, doesn't it? It is simple! **Some people never grow as followers of Jesus because, even though they have been freed for a life of love and service toward God, they choose to remain slaves to sin.** Others recognize the freedom we receive through Jesus' victory over sin and death in our lives must be used by responding to Jesus' salvation with loving obedience. I have been asked many times over the years why I think I have to obey God, why I think I always have to do the right thing. I don't think that I **have** to obey God or that I **have** to do the "right" thing. I **get** to obey God, and I **get** to do the right thing. I have never regretted obeying God and being a slave to Him. I have often regretted disobeying God and being a slave to sin. Thankfully, more and more in my life, I am recognizing the blessing of obeying God, which leads to growth. As I conform to the image of Jesus, growing becomes more and more natural.

In the end, whether we grow or not is a matter of commitment and choice. If you are growing—praise God! Continue to make yourself a slave to God. If you aren't growing, it is time to give up slavery to sin and hand the reins of life over to God. That single step guarantees growth in your life, so why not take it right now?

For the Questions For Discussion And Growth for
Slaves To Sin Or Righteousness go to page 117 now!

Questions For Discussion And Growth

Introduction: Stumbling Blocks Along The Way

What stumbling blocks and excuses have kept you from committing to growing as a follower of Jesus?

What do you need to do to commit to growing into the full stature of Jesus in your life?

To what are you committed in your life?

The Parable Of The Sower (Mark 4:1-9)

What kind of soil are you? What do you need to do to ensure that you are or become fertile soil?

What would it look like in your life to be producing "thirty, sixty or even a hundred times as much as was planted"?

Slaves To Sin Or Righteousness (Romans 6:1-18)

What impact does the Apostle Paul's analogy about our dying to sin and identifying with Jesus' death in our baptism have on you? Why?

Does Jesus' overcoming sin and death bring hope to you in the battle to overcome sin and to grow as His follower? Why or why not?

Who is your master right now: God or sin? What are you going to do to make sure God stays in charge?

9

Going Home

[Jesus said,] "³And if I go and prepare a place for you, I will come back and take you to be with me that you also may be where I am." (John 14:3 NIV)

Introduction:
The Perspective That Changes Everything

Everybody wants to go to heaven, but nobody wants to "get on the bus today." Contemporary, American Christianity has lost its emphasis on heaven and eternal life with God. The focus has become matters of the here and now. During my second year in seminary, as I interviewed for a student pastor position in a local church, I was asked, "What do you think about Jesus' second coming?" I responded by saying how important I believe it is for us to be ready for Jesus' return. I said that while we are here our goal ought to be to know Him, to become like Him and to live in such a way that others want to know Him and become like Him, too. Everyone on the committee looked at each other. Then they smiled. I asked them what was going on. They told me they had asked the same question of several other students. They had been told that the other students were not thinking much about Jesus' second coming, because there were far more important matters to address. Really? What is more important than being ready to face Jesus? I do not raise that question as one who sits under a tree praying every day waiting for Jesus' return. In fact, I take Jesus' words in the Lord's Prayer quite seriously, "Your kingdom come, your will be done on earth, as it is in heaven." (Matthew 6:10 NIV) Jesus wants us to be at least as concerned with bringing God's will to earth as we are of going to heaven! Yet, there can be no doubt that until our focus becomes abiding with Jesus for eternity we will never loosen our grip on the world. *Here's the perspective that changes everything: We are primarily citizens of heaven (God's Kingdom).* Everything else is secondary. Jesus told us to seek first the kingdom of heaven and its righteousness and everything else would be provided. The Apostle Paul was invincible as a missionary, because he did not care whether he lived or died. No one can control a person who is motivated by pleasing Jesus and being with Him beyond everything else. We now turn to four Scriptures that illuminate this perspective that changes everything.

For the Questions For Discussion And Growth for
Introduction: The Perspective That Changes Everything
go to page 129 now!

I Go To Prepare A Place (John 14:1-6)

That Jesus saw heaven as worthy of pursuit for our lives cannot be doubted. In His last hours with the disciples before His crucifixion, Jesus took the time to emphasize that His "leaving" was a good thing. One of the ways He did that was by telling them where He was going and what He was going to do when He got there:

[Jesus said] [1]"Do not let your hearts be troubled. Trust in God; trust also in me. [2]In my Father's house are many rooms; if it were not so, I would have told you. I am going there to prepare a place for you. [3]And if I go and prepare a place for you, I will come back and take you to be with me

120

that you also may be where I am. [4]You know the way to the place where I am going."

[5]Thomas said to him, "Lord, we don't know where you are going, so how can we know the way?"

[6]Jesus answered, "I am the way and the truth and the life. No one comes to the Father except through me. (John 14:1-6 NIV)

Jesus' words from John 14, are often spoken at funerals, and rightly so. When we pause to remember those who have died, considering their eternal home, what better words than these? First, Jesus comforted the disciples by reminding them to trust in God and Him. Since God and Jesus are one, this point should have been easy to digest, but it wasn't. Later in the passage, Philip showed the confusion of the group by asking Jesus to show them the "Father." Jesus' responded by saying, "If you know me, you know the Father."

After calling the disciples to trust Him, Jesus told them that He was going to heaven. He did not use those words. He told them He was going to His Father's house, and that the house has many rooms. Jesus underlined that if this were not true, He would have told them. Then He made the most amazing promise: If I go and prepare a place for you, I am coming back to take you there! Why? Jesus wants His followers to be with Him! In the end, Jesus' deepest desire is for abiding relationships with those who love Him. Jesus concluded His comments by saying that the disciples knew the way to the place he was going. Thomas was confused. The rest of the guys may have been confused as well, but only Thomas spoke: "Lord, we have no clue where you are going, so how can we know the way?" Jesus' response shows the inclusivity and the exclusivity of the Gospel. Jesus answered, "I am the way and the truth and the life. No one comes to the Father except through me." What an inclusive statement—anyone can come to the Father through Jesus! What an exclusive statement—no one can come to the Father except through

Jesus! The end of every Christian's life cycle is "going home." Our home is not here. Our home is heaven. Jesus is already preparing our "room." He will return and take us home one day. Jesus' statements rule out reincarnation. They rule out universal entrance into heaven for everyone by virtue of being alive. They rule out disintegrating into the dust from which we came. They rule out merging with the universe and becoming one with nothing.

Jesus' words take the reality, the certainty and the potential fear of death and turn them into the greatest blessing we will ever know. Some say this is a futile hope. Others say it is superstitious nonsense. It conflicts with every worldview except the biblical, Judeo-Christian one. From the standpoint of a biological life-cycle, every person is born, grows for a specified time and dies. If the person lives to be eighteen years old in our culture, that person is considered to be an adult. Then one day the person dies. The life cycle ends. The life cycle of a Christian has similarities and differences. We, too, are born, but then growth may stop. One day we die, but then life **does not** stop! That is the amazing difference. It is often said we ought to begin with the end in mind. Nowhere in life is that more important and true than when discussing the life cycle of a Christian!

For the Questions For Discussion And Growth for
I Go To Prepare A Place go to page 130 now!

For Me To Live Is Christ (Philippians 1:20-24)

The Apostle Paul held one of the boldest views of heaven ever. He constantly held the tension between desiring to go and be with Jesus and staying to tell more people about Him. He lived to equip more people to do the same. In our reading from Philippians 1, Paul makes it clear just how ready he was to be with Jesus at any moment:

²⁰I eagerly expect and hope that I will in no way be ashamed, but will have sufficient courage so that now as always Christ will be exalted in my body, whether by life or by death. ²¹For to me, to live is Christ and to die is gain. ²²If I am to go on living in the body, this will mean fruitful labor for me. Yet what shall I choose? I do not know! ²³I am torn between the two: I desire to depart and be with Christ, which is better by far; ²⁴but it is more necessary for you that I remain in the body. (Philippians 1:20-24 NIV)

Paul was in prison when he penned those words. He did not know whether he would live or die. He had faced death on many occasions and would face it again before he actually died to this life and went to be with the Lord. Philippians 1:21 has rung down through the ages as the absolute best attitude to hold toward life and death: *For to me, to live is Christ and to die is gain.* Amazing, isn't it? It says it all. If our lives are wrapped up in Jesus—so that whatever we do here and now is about Him—then, when we die, it will certainly be gain. In fact, can you not picture Jesus waiting for us to arrive so He can say, "Great job! You were incredible!"? Wouldn't that be perfect? Paul knew his daily life glorified Jesus. He knew his life was dedicated to knowing, loving and serving Jesus. He knew the moment he died to this life, he would be in the presence of Jesus. *How much better is that than being here?* That, my friends is the question. Do we really see dying as gain? Do we genuinely believe, as Paul did, that to die physically is gain because that is the doorway to spiritual life with Jesus forever?

Paul went on to tell of his dilemma. He wanted to go to heaven, which he said was better by far. (The original Greek, actually reads "much more better"!) Nevertheless, he knew there were those who needed him here. If he continued living, his "fruitful labor" could continue. If he died, he got a major promotion! That is what you call a win-win situation of epic proportions. That is what all of us who bear the name of Jesus have. The challenge is to live it. The

123

challenge is to recognize that whether we live or die is not the question. We **are** alive and we **are** going to die, unless Jesus returns first (which has always been my first choice!). The real question is *What are we doing right now to make certain the moment we meet Jesus is the best day of our eternity?* The answer is simple—not easy, but simple: Love God with all our hearts, souls, minds and strength, and love our neighbors as ourselves. How that gets lived out day by day is different for each of us. That it gets lived out is the key. As we do that, living **is** Christ and dying will most certainly be gain!

For the Questions For Discussion And Growth for
For Me To Live Is Christ go to pg. 130 now!

Grief And Hope (1 Thessalonians 4:13-14)

On February 15, 1988, Nancy, my wife, had a miscarriage. We had been married for nearly nine years and trying to have children for a number of them. She finally became pregnant, and we rejoiced in the hope that we would finally be parents. Then everything went wrong, and our first child died before being born. I was royally ticked off at God. As I sat alone in the hospital's emergency room waiting room, I thought of Scripture and tried to make sense of it all. Then the Scripture recounting King David and His first child born to Bathsheba came to mind. The child was sick when it was born and died after living only a short while. During the child's brief life, David fasted and prayed. He did not bathe or take care of himself. But when the child died, he got up, bathed and ate. His servants could not understand the logic. Why fast and pray until the child died and then act is if everything was okay after he did? David responded, "While the child was still alive, I fasted and wept. I thought, 'Who knows? The LORD may be gracious to me and let the child live.' [23]But now that he is dead, why should I fast? Can I bring him back again? I will go to him, but he will not return to me.'"" (2 Samuel 12:22-23 NIV) Those words comforted me in my grief. I know one day I will see our first child—in heaven. A week later, I was to preach a message titled "Grief and Hope" from 1 Thessalonians 4:13-14, the Scripture we consider here. That scripture also brought comfort. It reminded me that while Christians are not exempt from suffering, when one of our loved ones dies, we rejoice for our loved one; but grieve for our own loss. Here is how the Apostle Paul put it:

> ^{13}And now, dear brothers and sisters, we want you to know what will happen to the believers who have died so you will not grieve like people who have no hope. ^{14}For since we believe that Jesus died and was raised to life again, we also believe that when Jesus returns, God will bring back with him the believers who have died. (1 Thessalonians 4:13-14 NLT)

We do not grieve as the rest of people who have no hope. If you do not believe that Jesus went to prepare a place and that He is coming back for us, if you have no hope of the resurrection to everlasting life, then when someone dies they are gone—period. There is grief but no hope. That is **not** how it is for us. When someone dies, and that person has trusted Jesus as Savior and Lord, we know where we will find the person. We rejoice for their having received the "gain" Paul spoke of to the Christians in Philippi. Still, we grieve our loss for a time. One day we will be reunited with them in heaven. What an amazing moment that will be! In the mean time, we grieve the loss of those we love—in hope—knowing there is no greater blessing in life than living it eternally with Jesus.

For the Questions For Discussion And Growth for
Grief And Hope go to page 131 now!

Well Done (Matthew 25:14-15; 19-21; 24-30)

In our final Scripture Jesus tells us what the Kingdom of Heaven is like through a parable about a master and his three servants. Two of whom demonstrated themselves faithful. The third did not. Let us look at Jesus' words and consider the implications for our lives.

> [Jesus said] [14]"Again, the Kingdom of Heaven can be illustrated by the story of a man going on a long trip. He called together his servants and entrusted his money to them while he was gone. [15]He gave five bags of silver to one, two bags of silver to another, and one bag of silver to the last— dividing it in proportion to their abilities. He then left on his trip.'" (Matthew 25:14-15 NLT)

Notice the master entrusted his wealth to his servants while he was gone, but he did not divide the money equally. He gave five-eighths of it to the first servant, one-fourth of it to the second servant and one-eighth of it to the third servant. Why? We are told the master understood the servants' abilities and divided the wealth up accordingly. While that may seem unfair, Jesus recognized that we are all "differently-abled" and to treat us the same would be to ignore the uniqueness with which He created us. In verses 16-18, we are told that the first two servants doubled the portion of their master's wealth entrusted to them while the third servant buried his portion in the ground. Then we read:

> [19]"After a long time their master returned from his trip and called them to give an account of how they had used his money. [20]The servant to whom he had entrusted the five bags of silver came forward with five more and said, 'Master, you gave me five bags of silver to invest, and I have earned five more.'"

> [21]"The master was full of praise. 'Well done, my good and faithful servant. You have been faithful in handling this small amount, so now I will give you many more

responsibilities. Let's celebrate together!'" (Matthew 25:19-21 NLT)

When the master returned, he required an accounting of each servant. Remember, Jesus was telling a parable of what the Kingdom of Heaven is like, so we must assume that we will one day give an accounting of how we managed the resources Jesus has entrusted to us throughout our lives, as well. The first servant did well. He doubled his master's wealth. The master was pleased. He responded by saying, "Well done, my good and faithful servant. You have been faithful in handling this small amount, so now I will give you many more responsibilities. Let's celebrate together!" Notice the affirmation of the servant: He was called good and faithful. What more could God say to us when we enter heaven than that! The master called the sum entrusted to the first servant "small." Actually, five talents was a tremendous sum of money; but to the One who holds the universe in His hand, it was, indeed, small. The master offers a vital principle: You have been faithful with little—so I'll make you responsible for more! Some see heaven as a place of perpetual rest or harp playing. Jesus' parable presents it as a place of responsibility—increasing responsibility for those who have been faithful on earth. While telling the servant that his responsibilities would be increasing, the master concludes by inviting him to celebrate with him. Heaven is a place of celebration!

In verses 22-23, we are told that the second servant was affirmed in the same way as the first, because he, too, was faithful. Then we read:

> [24]"Then the servant with the one bag of silver came and said, 'Master, I knew you were a harsh man, harvesting crops you didn't plant and gathering crops you didn't cultivate. [25]I was afraid I would lose your money, so I hid it in the earth. Look, here is your money back.'"

26"But the master replied, 'You wicked and lazy servant! If you knew I harvested crops I didn't plant and gathered crops I didn't cultivate, 27why didn't you deposit my money in the bank? At least I could have gotten some interest on it.'"

28"Then he ordered, 'Take the money from this servant, and give it to the one with the ten bags of silver. 29To those who use well what they are given, even more will be given, and they will have an abundance. But from those who do nothing, even what little they have will be taken away. 30Now throw this useless servant into outer darkness, where there will be weeping and gnashing of teeth.'" (Matthew 25:24-30 NLT)

The third servant saw the master differently than the first two. They trusted his generosity enough to risk what they had received from him in order to gain more. The third servant was afraid of the master and did nothing with his wealth. As we see from the master's response, the third servant's fear was not borne out of reverence or respect. The master's response was extremely critical. He called the servant wicked and lazy. He asked why the servant, knowing of his master's harshness, did not at least deposit the money in a bank so he would gain interest. The servant's money is taken from him and given to the first servant, and a new principle is added: The faithful ones will receive more, and the ones who are not faithful will lose even what they have. Instead of inviting the third servant to celebrate, he is thrown into "outer darkness" where there will be weeping and gnashing of teeth—this is certainly **not** heaven.

Jesus makes it clear that heaven has an opposing destination: hell. He makes it clear that trusting the master is the prerequisite for entering heaven. He makes it clear, that while He is the one who gives the wealth, those who use it well will be rewarded well. What a very practical image of heaven. Some resist viewing heaven as a place of rewards as if seeking reward is wrong. The reality is in being faithful to Jesus here on earth we are sowing rewards in heaven. The rewards are not our goal. They are the consequence of our faithfulness. May we live here and now in such a way that we, too, will one day hear the words, "Well done, good and faithful servant."

For the Questions For Discussion And Growth for
Well Done go to page 132 now!

Questions For Discussion And Growth

Introduction: The Perspective That Changes Everything

What place do thoughts about heaven fill in your daily thinking? Is it something you consider often or seldom?

Do you agree or disagree that the perspective that changes everything is that we are primarily citizens of heaven? Why?

What does it mean to you to live out these words of the Lord's Prayer, "Your kingdom come, Your will be done on earth as it is in heaven?"

I Go To Prepare A Place (John 14:1-6)

Why do you suppose the disciples were so clueless about what Jesus was saying in John 14:1-6?

How do you picture heaven? How do Jesus' words in John 14:1-6 influence that picture?

Why do you suppose that Jesus made such an exclusive/inclusive statement about being the only way to heaven?

For Me To Live is Christ (Philippians 1:20-24)

Why do you think Paul could hold such an amazing attitude toward living and dying?

Do you hold the same attitude? Why or why not?

What one thing do you take away from this Scripture that will help you live more faithfully and be better prepared to "go home"?

Grief And Hope (1 Thessalonians 4:13-18)

When someone you love dies, are you able to hold an attitude of hopeful grief? Why or why not?

How does Paul's description of what happens after we die add to your understanding of what it is like to "go home"?

Well Done (Matthew 25:14-30)

Why do you suppose that Jesus used the story of the master and the three servants as an image of heaven?

What do we learn from the first two servants?

What do we learn from the third servant?

10

Leaving a Legacy

⁹Whatever you have learned or received or heard from me, or seen in me—put it into practice. And the God of peace will be with you. (Philippians 4:9 NLT)

Introduction: Paying It Forward

Back in the fall of 2000, a movie hit the theaters titled *Pay It Forward*. The gist of the movie is that a boy was challenged by his social studies teacher to come up with an idea that would change the world. The boy's idea was that when someone did something good in your life, instead of "paying them back," you "pay it forward." Paying it forward meant doing three good deeds for three other people. The idea succeeded beyond the boy's wildest dreams. Although the movie ends on an extremely sad note as the boy is killed while attempting to continue to pay it forward, its basic premise forms the basis for our final topic. As followers of Jesus, we cannot pay Him back for securing our salvation through His death on the cross. What He calls us to do, in a manner of speaking, is to pay it forward. He once told the disciples, "Freely you have received, freely give." That is the pay-it-forward concept in action. Jesus' greatest desire for each of us is to come to know and trust Him as Savior and Lord. As a result, He calls us to reach out to others with the gift of salvation in His name. As we do that, we leave behind a legacy of transformed lives. The idea of leaving a legacy is not new. Down through the ages people have sought to leave some kind of indelible mark on history. Some have done it through inventions that have moved humanity forward. Others have done it through conquering distant lands. Jesus did it by giving His life away to redeem the world and investing in the lives of a handful of followers who took His new way of life to the world in word and action.

What kind of legacy are you building? How will you be remembered by those closest to you? Sometimes people get at the idea of legacy by asking, "What do you want engraved on your tombstone?" I have thought about that over the years, and have come up with an answer: **He served Jesus, and even his wife and daughters loved him.** Some might wonder about the second half of the statement. I include it because I have seen too many pastors' families in which the spouse and children take a backseat not only to God (as they should), but to everyone else in the church as well (as they should not). I have learned over the years that serving the church is not always serving God. I pray that at least part of my legacy will be to help others—pastors and other believers alike—to learn that as well. As you reflect on legacy in this closing chapter, I pray you will take some time to consider what you want on your tombstone and what your legacy will be.

For the Questions For Discussion And Growth for
Introduction: Paying It Forward go to page 146 now!

The Legacy Starts At Home (Deuteronomy 6:1-9; Ephesians 6:4)

Often when we think of legacy, we think of something big: We want to find a cure for cancer, or take the gospel to an unreached people or set a world record that will never be broken. What about this:

Passing on the faith in Jesus you have received to your children? Not everyone who reads this is married or has biological or adopted children. That does not mean you cannot share your faith in Jesus with the next generation. After all, as followers of Jesus, we are members of an extended family, and spiritual infants can be born into it every day. All children need to receive our faith in Jesus so they might also believe and receive salvation in His name. Then, those children need to be raised in the faith that they may one day become spiritual "parents" and by God's grace bear spiritual "newborns," as well.

When God established the Law among the people of Israel, He made certain such a legacy would be normative among His people. Moses recorded these commands of God to show us all what we must do for the generations coming after us:

> [1]"These are the commands, decrees, and regulations that the LORD your God commanded me to teach you. You must obey them in the land you are about to enter and occupy, [2]and you and your children and grandchildren must fear the LORD your God as long as you live. If you obey all his decrees and commands, you will enjoy a long life. [3]Listen closely, Israel, and be careful to obey. Then all will go well with you, and you will have many children in the land flowing with milk and honey, just as the LORD, the God of your ancestors, promised you. (Deuteronomy 6:1-3 NLT)

First, God tells the people they must obey Him in the land they are about to enter—the Promised Land. He tells them not only they but also their children and their grandchildren must fear the Lord as long as they live. A promise comes with the command: Obedience will bring an abundance of children and blessing, material and otherwise. We have not yet reached the point in the passage where the Israelites are commanded to pass the legacy on to their children, but we see God's clear intention: Our children, our grandchildren and our great-grandchildren are to be part of the people known as God's family. All too often, as our children grow they are being exposed to alternative worldviews and given freedoms that they are ill-equipped to handle. Why? In many cases it is because we have failed to teach them, encourage them and show them what it means to follow Jesus--to think like Him, to act like Him and to become more and more fully devoted and developing followers of Him--so they don't.

> [4]"Listen, O Israel! The LORD is our God, the LORD alone. [5]And you must love the LORD your God with all your heart, all your soul, and all your strength. [6]And you must commit yourselves whole-heartedly to these commands that I am giving you today. [7]Repeat them again and again to your children. Talk about them when you are at home and when you are on the road, when you are going to bed and when you are getting up. [8]Tie them to your hands and wear them on your forehead as reminders. [9]Write them on the doorposts of your house and on your gates. (Deuteronomy 6:4-9 NLT)

God established that He alone is God and we must love Him **first**. Next, we must commit ourselves to following His commands. Then we must repeat them again and again and again to our children. We are told we are always to be talking with our children about God and His ways. This does not mean brainwashing or badgering our children into compliance. It means living the love of Jesus Christ in our words and actions in such a way that our children naturally receive Him as their Savior and Lord. Our children will not always believe what we say, but they will always believe what we do. If I tell my children I love them but do not show them daily, they will not believe me no matter how many times I tell them. On the other hand, even though I may not always tell my children I love them, if I act in their best interest, investing time with them to teach them God's ways, they will know I love them. *The best of all possible legacies for our children is to both tell them* **and** *show them that we love them.* When our words and actions coincide the hypocrisy factor in our lives is zero, and that is what we want. I do not want my children to walk away from church as I did saying, "They are all a bunch of hypocrites and I don't need them." I do not want anyone's children doing that. So, if we want to leave our children legacies of loving God and living in and for Him, we must love Him, obey His commands and teach them to our children with our words and our lives. That only happens as we grow in our own walks with Jesus, as we move toward maturity in Him.

Let us turn now to a brief instruction to fathers, written by the Apostle Paul to the church at Ephesus: "⁴Fathers, do not provoke your children to anger by the way you treat them. Rather, bring them up with the discipline and instruction that comes from the Lord" (Ephesians 6:4 NLT).

Some translations have substituted the word *Parents* for the word *Fathers*, but Paul was not addressing parents in general. He was addressing male parents—fathers—in specific. He did that because he was a man, and he knew that men are not naturally nurturing. He knew that without even trying we can provoke our children to anger by the ways we treat them. We mean well, but we often overindulge or over control them, and they do not respond well. Nor should they. We only try to control the people and things in life that we do not trust. That means every controlling initiative we take toward our children provokes anger. It tells them we do not trust them. Am I saying we ought never to control our children? Of course not! We set boundaries for them and stick to them—that is discipline—but only if the boundaries are for their good and not ours. We must trust our children as much as they show us they deserve to be trusted. As they mature, we move from being in charge to being available. Most dads I see these days are as guilty of indulging their children as of controlling them. When we give our children everything they want when they want it, we turn them into masters. We become their slaves. Since our ultimate goal is for them to become slaves of God, not slaves of sin, we do well to be certain that when we indulge them it is in the love of the Lord and with our time because to children time **is** love. Buying them more stuff and getting them involved in all the things we missed in life does them no favors. It promotes the very obstacles to growing in Jesus that we hope to avoid in our own lives.

I invest so much time here, because it is so much better to invest time in our children when they are growing than to invest time in trying to fix them when they are grown. I have made many, many mistakes as a father and have provoked my children to anger on more than a few occasions. In it all, though, they have known that I love them and that I always will. I learned that from Jesus, who is especially fond of me, even when I am disobedient. He is especially fond of you as well, even when you are disobedient. Disobedience is not His preference for us, just as it is not our preference for our children. The difference is Jesus never asks us to do anything merely for the sake of controlling us or making Himself feel good. If we are to leave legacies that transform our children, we must be in the process of transformation ourselves. We must be living and growing in Jesus. As they see that, they will want to have it in their lives, too. Nothing is more contagious than a life truly devoted to God! Fathers we need to step up to the plate and rear our children—all of them—in the discipline and instruction of the Lord.

For the Questions For Discussion And Growth for
The Legacy Starts At Home go to page 147 now!

With Me (Mark 3:13-19)

Many years ago, I attended a seminar hosted by Dr. Stan Ott. He was pastoring in the South Hills of Pittsburgh at the time, and one of the principles he offered was the "With Me Principle." Stan had gleaned this principle from Mark 3:13-19, Jesus' calling of the twelve disciples. The With Me Principle is fairly straight-forward: Never minister alone. What does the With Me Principle have to do with legacy? Everything, as we will soon see.

> [13]Afterward Jesus went up on a mountain and called out the ones he wanted to go with him. And they came to him. [14]Then he appointed twelve of them and called them his apostles. They were to accompany him, and he would send them out to preach, [15]giving them authority to cast out demons. [16]Here are their names:
>
> Simon (whom he named Peter), [17]James and John (the sons of Zebedee, but Jesus nicknamed them "Sons of Thunder"), [18]Andrew,
>
> Philip, Bartholomew, Matthew, Thomas, James (son of Alphaeus), Thaddaeus, Simon (the zealot), [19]Judas Iscariot (who later betrayed him). (Mark 3:13-19 NLT)

Jesus called twelve and appointed them as apostles. Apostles are literally people who are sent out with a purpose; but before Jesus sent them out, He called them to "go with Him," to be with Him. Eventually, eleven of those twelve men would serve Jesus faithfully—ten of them to their deaths, but first they would be with Him. Why is that so important? The best way to establish a legacy with people is by being with them! I learned to do pastoral calls by being with Andy Wiegand. I learned to preach by being with a number of good preachers when they preached, hearing the good points, noting the not so good ones and recognizing that God had gifted me in ways that were like **and** unlike any of them. I thank God, though, that the models I was with over the years were passionate about Jesus and willing to invest time in being with me.

If you have not been intentional about investing your life in being with others, starting with your own children--if you have any--you will have a greater challenge in leaving the kind of legacy Jesus calls us to leave. Yes, some of us are more outgoing than others. Yes, it is easier for some of us to be with people than it is for others. I am not asking you to invest in others so you will be comfortable. I am asking you to do it so you will be like Jesus and so the others you are with can become like Him, too. The twelve men Jesus chose were not like Him, and they were not like each other. In fact, it is a true wonder that Matthew, a tax collector and collaborator with Rome, could even be in the same room with Simon (the zealot), who belonged to a radical group that wanted to overthrow Rome. Jesus did not choose the men to be with Him for His benefit, but for theirs. The legacy he left in their lives has influenced the world for nearly 2,000 years—one generation at a time. Christianity could have ended in any generation during those 2,000 years. It continues because men and women have determined to take people with them, to teach, train, encourage and hold them accountable. Most of those people are unknown to the world. To the one who was able to be with them, though, they were of infinite value because, through them, that one entered eternity! What greater legacy can there be than that? It all starts with people who know Jesus taking others alongside of them, loving them and showing them into the Kingdom.

For the Questions For Discussion And Growth for
With Me go to page 147 now!

What You Have Seen In Me (Philippians 4:8-9)

The words we are about to read from the Apostle Paul are an extension of the With Me Principle. Paul not only served as a mentor to Silas, Timothy, Titus and others, he also served as a role model and teacher for many. While mentoring is crucial in our growth and development as followers of Jesus, sometimes our influence takes the form of modeling for and teaching groups of people. In Philippians 4

Paul offers instructions about the kinds of things with which we ought to fill our minds. Then he gets personal:

> [8]Finally, brothers, whatever is true, whatever is noble, whatever is right, whatever is pure, whatever is lovely, whatever is admirable—if anything is excellent or praiseworthy—think about such things. [9]Whatever you have learned or received or heard from me, or seen in me—put it into practice. And the God of peace will be with you. (Philippians 4:8-9 NIV)

Without a doubt, we will grow in our walk with Jesus if we think about that which is true, noble, right, pure, lovely, admirable, excellent and praiseworthy. Living in a world filled with cesspool images as we do, dwelling on goodness provides a much needed environment for growth. After offering helpful instruction in a general way, Paul says, "Do you remember what you have learned from me, heard from me or seen me do? Do you remember those things? Healing that sick person? Preaching in the marketplace? Praying and fasting for God's salvation to come to this city? Here is what you do next: Put those things into practice yourselves." Paul's life was a legacy for the Christians in Philippi, Ephesus, Thessalonica and dozens of other places. *The greatest legacy we can offer is ourselves, fully devoted to Jesus!* When we do that, when we **are** that, when we live that, people's lives are changed. Some of the most humbling words I have heard over the years are, "Something you said changed my life." "When you were our youth pastor, I accepted Jesus." "It's refreshing to see a man who practices what he preaches." When I hear those things, knowing how far short I fall of the full stature of Jesus at times, I thank God that He uses me, warts and all! He will use you, warts and all, as well. All it takes is all you are and all you have! Give it to Jesus, and He will give it back much better than it was when you gave it to Him. What kind of legacy do you want to leave? There is none better than a life that leads others to Jesus!

For the Questions For Discussion And Growth for
What You Have Seen In Me go to page 148 now!

Imitate Me (1 Corinthians 10:31-11:1)

Of all the things the Apostle Paul ever wrote, the words below are some of the most challenging:

> [31]So whether you eat or drink or whatever you do, do it all for the glory of God. [32]Do not cause anyone to stumble, whether Jews, Greeks or the church of God—[33]even as I try to please everybody in every way. For I am not seeking my own good but the good of many, so that they may be saved. [11:1]Follow my example, as I follow the example of Christ. (1 Corinthians 10:31-11:1 NIV)

"Follow my example, as I follow the example of Christ." Wow! That is when you know you are fully grown as a follower of Jesus. Paul was not saying he had arrived. In fact, you could read it as, "Follow my example, but only when I am following the example of Christ." Paul had matured spiritually to the point he could appeal to his life as an example for others to follow. What an incredible legacy! What more can we do than be living, walking, breathing models of Jesus Christ for others to see and imitate? Paul's initial words are details but important details: Whatever we do—**whatever** we do—do it all for the glory of God. When we do that, we will not cause anyone to stumble. That is one of the most important goals in my life, being a model worthy of following because I am following Jesus. I do not want to cause anyone to stumble. I know I have caused people to stumble in the past because I have not been perfect—and still am not perfect. I no longer lose sleep over becoming **better** because I know I will never be better than I am right

142

now. My prayer is not to be better but to **love Jesus more** and to **let the Holy Spirit shine His light through me more** so people will see Jesus in me and not me. Paul's next to last statement is a statement of legacy: "For I am not seeking my own good but the good of many, so that they may be saved." When we get there in our lives, when we are more concerned about the good of the unsaved many than about our own good, we will leave a legacy of souls transformed for eternity. Jesus told us to store up our treasure in heaven, and the only treasure of heaven is people! Paul understood that and devoted his life to seeing it become a reality. Our lives count most when we are giving them away in the name of Jesus, so others will come to know Him, too.

For the Questions For Discussion And Growth for
Imitate Me go to page 148 now!

All The World (Matthew 28:18-20)

Our last Scripture is Jesus' Great Commission, His sending forth of the believers to transform the world by making disciples:

> [18]Jesus came and told his disciples, "I have been given all authority in heaven and on earth. [19]Therefore, go and make disciples of all the nations, baptizing them in the name of the Father and the Son and the Holy Spirit. [20]Teach these new disciples to obey all the commands I have given you. And be sure of this: I am with you always, even to the end of the age." (Matthew 28:18-20 NLT)

When Jesus rose from the dead, He appeared to the disciples over a period of forty days. When those forty days came to an end, He appeared one last time and commissioned the disciples to true greatness. What do I mean by that? He commissioned them to tell **the entire** world about Him, not just to **tell** them but also to **make disciples** of them. The only verb in the entire commission in the

143

original Greek text is "make disciples." In English, it looks like there are several more: go, baptize and teach. Each of those words in the Greek text is a participle, meaning they take their action from the main verb. It is as if Jesus said, "While you're going (because I **assume** you will be going), make disciples of **all** the nations, baptizing them—since that is the response of those who become disciples—in the name of the Father and of the Son and of the Holy Spirit, teaching them to obey all my commands, because that is one of the best ways to make disciples. As you are doing all of that, remember this: I **am** with you always, even to the end of the age.

The world tells us the way to leave a legacy is to become a millionaire or a billionaire, to have a hospital or a school named after us or to write a book that everyone will read. Jesus tells us the way to leave a legacy is to make disciples of the entire world! The greatest thing about that is, once we make disciples, they can make disciples, who will make disciples.... And one day **all** of those disciples will live together in heaven for eternity. **That** is definitely a legacy.

For the Questions For Discussion And Growth for
All The World go to page 149 now!

The Life Cycle Continues

I told Emmy, our younger daughter, that I was writing a book. She asked me what it was it was about. I said, "The life cycle of a Christian."

She thought about that for a moment and said, "The life of a Christian isn't a cycle. It has a beginning, a middle and an end; and then it goes on forever in heaven. That's not a cycle. It's a timeline."

I said, "It's not a timeline, because it goes on forever. Once we die time doesn't matter and has no meaning." She went to bed shortly after that conversation, but the next morning she called downstairs to my study and said, "Daddy, here's how the Christian life is a cycle. A person is born again. They grow up as a follower of Jesus. Then they lead someone else to Jesus, and that person has a new beginning. That's where the cycle starts over again." Amen! I thanked her for the insight and told her I would use her comments at the end of the book, because the final chapter is about leaving a legacy. Until we leave a legacy of another disciple who will be born again and grow so he or she can make another disciple who will be born again and grow, there is no life cycle of a Christian. Are you part of the life cycle of a Christian? Have you helped someone start the life that only Jesus gives? One of the best parts of the process of growing up into the full stature of Jesus is that along the way, we have opportunities to help others become part of the family, part of the cycle. As we mature, we come to understand that part of our new nature is to tell others about Jesus, to show them Jesus, to invite them to be part of the family and to rejoice when they are born again.

One of my favorite movies is *It's a Wonderful Life.* If you know the movie, you know the hero is George Bailey, a man with big dreams about going places, designing major buildings and making millions. The problem is he never gets to leave Bedford Falls, the little town where he was born. He never gets to build things, just the lives of people all around him. At the end of the movie when George is in trouble and thinks the world would have been better off if he had never been born, he has the opportunity to see that the world would **not** have been better off without him. After this revelation, he gladly decides to go home, turn himself in and go to jail to pay a penalty his uncle should have paid. Instead, when he gets home the people George has helped throughout his life help him. The movie closes with George reading a quote from a "friend," an angel named Clarence: "Remember, George: No man is a failure who has friends." I love the movie because it shows that one person, even an unknown person, can make an incredible difference. When that one person is growing as Jesus' follower and helping others to become and grow as Jesus' followers, the difference is **eternal**! May you recognize the wonder of life in Jesus day-by-day and, in that recognition, reach out to someone else who needs to know Him. Only then does the life cycle continue. Only then!

For the Questions For Discussion And Growth for
The Life Cycle Continues go to page 150 now!

Questions For Discussion And Growth

Introduction: Paying It Forward

Do you see the idea of paying it forward as a good way to introduce the concept of legacy? Why or why not?

What would you like to have engraved on your tombstone?

The Legacy Starts At Home (Deuteronomy 6:1-9; Ephesians 6:4)

If you could leave a legacy to humanity of curing a terminal disease, but it meant your own children would be ignored, would it be worth it? Why or why not?

What is the most important action point you take away from Deuteronomy 6:1-9 and Ephesians 6:4?

With Me (Mark 3:13-19)

With whom are you applying the With Me principle among your family and friends?

How intentional are you about applying the With Me principle beyond your circle of family and friends?

Who applied the With Me principle in your life that has made a lasting difference? How have you paid that forward in your life?

What You Have Seen In Me (Philippians 4:8-9)

How would you be different if you reflected only on things that were true, noble, right, pure, lovely, admirable, excellent and praiseworthy?

If people listened to what you said and watched what you did day in and day out, what kind of legacy would they receive?

Imitate Me (1 Corinthians 10:31-11:1)

On a scale of 1-10 (10 being high); where would you rate yourself on being worthy of being imitated by others?

How important is it to you to leave a legacy of souls saved? What are you doing to see that legacy become a reality?

All The World (Matthew 28:16-20)

What is the significance to you of Jesus' primary command in the Great Commission being to make disciples?

What will it take for you to become an intentional disciple maker so your legacy will be eternal?

The Life Cycle Continues

List three to five people you know who don't know Jesus as Savior and Lord.

      1)

      2)

      3)

      4)

      5)

What can you do to help them come to know Jesus? What will you do?

APPENDIX

Bibliography of Works Cited

The first five works cited below, would form the beginning of a good collection of books for your growth as a follower of Jesus.

The final two, were mentioned in passing; Brunner because of his comment on God not being "illogical," but alogical; and Erikson, because of his description of the stages of psycho-social development.

Change Your Heart, Change Your Life by Dr. Gary Smalley, Thomas Nelson Publishing, 2007.

Rick Warren's Bible Study Methods: Twelve Ways You Can Unlock God's Word by Rick Warren, Zondervan/Harper Collins Publishing, 2006.

Experiencing God by Dr. Henry Blackaby, Broadman & Holman Publishers, 1994.

The Normal Christian Life by Watchman Nee, Tyndale House Publishers, first published 1957.

Sit, Walk, Stand by Watchman Nee, Christian Literature Crusade, first published 1957.

Our Faith by Emil Brunner, Charles Scribner's Sons, 1936.

Identity: Youth and Crisis by Erik H. Erikson, W.W. Norton and Company, 1968.

Additional Copies of

Life Cycle of a Christian
A User's Guide to Life After Rebirth

For you, your home group, or church

May be purchased for

$12.00 each – Single Copies
$10.00 each -- Ten or More Copies
$8.50 each – Fifty or More Copies
Plus Shipping/Delivery and Tax

By contacting

Dr. Chris Marshall
CMarsh1957@aol.com
724-766-1965
447 Leasureville Road
Cabot, PA 16023

Thank you for reading *Life Cycle of a Christian*. If you have any questions, comments or suggestions to pass along to Dr. Marshall, please feel free to contact him at CMarsh1957@aol.com.